OPPOSING
VIEWPOINTS®
SERIES

Eating Disorders

Other Books of Related Interest:

Opposing Viewpoints Series

Food

Obesity

At Issue Series

Anorexia

Bulimia

Can Diets Be Harmful?

"Congress shall make no law ... abridging the freedom of speech, or of the press."

First Amendment to the U.S. Constitution

The basic foundation of our democracy is the First Amendment guarantee of freedom of expression. The Opposing Viewpoints series is dedicated to the concept of this basic freedom and the idea that it is more important to practice it than to enshrine it.

Eating Disorders

Viqi Wagner, Book Editor

GREENHAVEN PRESS
An imprint of Thomson Gale, a part of The Thomson Corporation

THOMSON
————*————
GALE

Detroit • New York • San Francisco • New Haven, Conn. • Waterville, Maine • London

THOMSON

✳ ™

GALE

Christine Nasso, *Publisher*
Elizabeth Des Chenes, *Managing Editor*

© 2007 Thomson Gale, a part of The Thomson Corporation.

Thomson and Star logo are trademarks and Gale and Greenhaven Press are registered trademarks used herein under license.

For more information, contact:
Greenhaven Press
27500 Drake Rd.
Farmington Hills, MI 48331-3535
Or you can visit our Internet site at http://www.gale.com

Cover photograph reproduced by permission of freephotos.com.

LIBRARY OF CONGRESS CATALOGING-IN-PUBLICATION DATA

Eating disorders / Viqi Wagner, book editor.
   p. cm. -- (Opposing viewpoints)
   Includes bibliographical references and index.
   ISBN-13: 978-0-7377-3348-8 (hardcover)
   ISBN-13: 978-0-7377-3349-5 (pbk.)
   1. Eating disorders--Juvenile literature. I. Wagner, Viqi, 1953-
   RC552.E18E2821133 2007
   616.85'26--dc22

                                                    2007007382

ISBN-10: 0-7377-3348-9 (hardcover)
ISBN-10: 0-7377-3349-7 (pbk.)

Printed in the United States of America
10 9 8 7 6 5 4 3 2 1

Contents

Chapter 1: Are Eating Disorders a Serious Problem?

Chapter 2: What Causes Eating Disorders?

Chapter 3: What Role Does the Internet Play in Eating Disorders?

Chapter 4: How Should Eating Disorders Be Treated?

Why Consider Opposing Viewpoints?

> *"The only way in which a human being can make some approach to knowing the whole of a subject is by hearing what can be said about it by persons of every variety of opinion and studying all modes in which it can be looked at by every character of mind. No wise man ever acquired his wisdom in any mode but this."*
>
> John Stuart Mill

In our media-intensive culture it is not difficult to find differing opinions. Thousands of newspapers and magazines and dozens of radio and television talk shows resound with differing points of view. The difficulty lies in deciding which opinion to agree with and which "experts" seem the most credible. The more inundated we become with differing opinions and claims, the more essential it is to hone critical reading and thinking skills to evaluate these ideas. Opposing Viewpoints books address this problem directly by presenting stimulating debates that can be used to enhance and teach these skills. The varied opinions contained in each book examine many different aspects of a single issue. While examining these conveniently edited opposing views, readers can develop critical thinking skills such as the ability to compare and contrast authors' credibility, facts, argumentation styles, use of persuasive techniques, and other stylistic tools. In short, the Opposing Viewpoints series is an ideal way to attain the higher-level thinking and reading skills so essential in a culture of diverse and contradictory opinions.

In addition to providing a tool for critical thinking, Opposing Viewpoints books challenge readers to question their own strongly held opinions and assumptions. Most people form their opinions on the basis of upbringing, peer pressure, and personal, cultural, or professional bias. By reading carefully balanced opposing views, readers must directly confront new ideas as well as the opinions of those with whom they disagree. This is not to simplistically argue that everyone who reads opposing views will—or should—change his or her opinion. Instead, the series enhances readers' understanding of their own views by encouraging confrontation with opposing ideas. Careful examination of others' views can lead to the readers' understanding of the logical inconsistencies in their own opinions, perspective on why they hold an opinion, and the consideration of the possibility that their opinion requires further evaluation.

Evaluating Other Opinions

To ensure that this type of examination occurs, Opposing Viewpoints books present all types of opinions. Prominent spokespeople on different sides of each issue as well as well-known professionals from many disciplines challenge the reader. An additional goal of the series is to provide a forum for other, less-known, or even unpopular viewpoints. The opinion of an ordinary person who has had to make the decision to cut off life support from a terminally ill relative, for example, may be just as valuable and provide just as much insight as a medical ethicist's professional opinion. The editors have two additional purposes in including these less-known views. One, the editors encourage readers to respect others' opinions—even when not enhanced by professional credibility. It is only by reading or listening to and objectively evaluating others' ideas that one can determine whether they are worthy of consideration. Two, the inclusion of such viewpoints encourages the important critical thinking skill of objectively evaluating an author's credentials and bias. This evaluation will illuminate an author's reasons for taking a particular stance on an issue and will aid in readers' evaluation of the author's ideas.

It is our hope that these books will give readers a deeper understanding of the issues debated and an appreciation of the complexity of even seemingly simple issues when good and honest people disagree. This awareness is particularly important in a democratic society such as ours in which people enter into public debate to determine the common good. Those with whom one disagrees should not be regarded as enemies but rather as people whose views deserve careful examination and may shed light on one's own.

Thomas Jefferson once said that "difference of opinion leads to inquiry, and inquiry to truth." Jefferson, a broadly educated man, argued that "if a nation expects to be ignorant and free . . . it expects what never was and never will be." As individuals and as a nation, it is imperative that we consider the opinions of others and examine them with skill and discernment. The Opposing Viewpoints series is intended to help readers achieve this goal.

David L. Bender and Bruno Leone,
Founders

Introduction

"When does 'normal' dieting, or 'normal' overeating, stop being normal and cross the line into an eating disorder? It is important to recognize that many, many people suffer from conflicted relationships with their eating. However, there are degrees of suffering and degrees of danger to health, with clinically diagnosable eating disorders inflicting the most of each."

—*Terese Katz,*
"Women, Food, and Eating Disorders"

A merica in the twenty-first century is an image-conscious society obsessed with physical health and beauty. There is nothing objectionable about losing weight and getting more exercise to reduce the risk of obesity-related disease and to feel better about oneself—doctors and government agencies encourage just that. The problem, critics charge, is that most Americans are distressed by medical and government recommendations for optimum weight and calorie intake: The majority eat more and weigh more than the guidelines say they should, while many others eat less and weigh less in pursuit of prevailing cultural ideals of beauty, especially female beauty, simplistically summarized as "thinner is better." The result is a national preoccupation with and anxiety over losing weight and chronic dissatisfaction with one's appearance. According to eating disorders specialist Margo Maine, 78 percent of eighteen-year-old girls are unhappy with their bodies and the number-one wish of girls ages eleven to seventeen is to lose weight. According to the American Obesity Association, consumers spend $30 billion per year trying to lose weight or avoid weight gain, the majority of Americans have unhealthy eating habits, and at any given time 40 percent of women and 25 percent of men are on a diet.

When preoccupation with body image and food restriction is taken to the extreme, it is no longer a reflection of cultural norms or a personality quirk but an abnormal condition generally called an eating disorder (ED). That's where agreement ends; significant controversy exists over how widespread and serious EDs are, how EDs are triggered, and how abnormal behaviors should be treated. Debate over all of these issues hinges, however, on a more basic controversy: How should eating disorders be defined? When most Americans have unhealthy eating habits to begin with, what exactly is an eating disorder?

Because the basic human drive for food originates in the emotional centers of the brain, eating disorders have traditionally been classified as psychiatric illnesses even though they have dangerous, potentially life-threatening physical effects. Since 1980, the criteria for the diagnosis of an eating disorder have been defined in the *Diagnostic and Statistical Manual* of the American Psychiatric Association, known as *DSM-IV*, now in its fourth revision.

There are two recognized eating disorder diagnoses. The better known disorder is anorexia nervosa, defined by five criteria:

1. Refusal to maintain body weight at or above a minimally normal weight for age and height (e.g., . . . body weight less than 85% of that expected).

2. Intense fear of gaining weight or becoming fat, even though underweight.

3. Disturbance in the way in which one's body weight or shape is experienced, . . . or denial of the seriousness of the current low body weight.

4. Self-evaluation is unduly influenced by body shape and weight.

5. In postmenarchal females, amenorrhea, i.e., the absence of at least three consecutive [menstrual] cycles. Anorexia nervosa is further subdivided into two types: restricting type, in which the person does not regularly binge or purge (i.e., induce vomiting or misuse laxatives, diuretics, or enemas), and binge-eating/purging type, in which the person does regularly binge or purge.

The second official eating disorder diagnosis is bulimia nervosa, defined by four criteria:

1. Recurrent episodes of binge eating . . . characterized by both of the following: 1) Eating, in a discrete period of time (e.g., within any 2-hour period), an amount of food that is definitely larger than most people would eat. . . . 2) A sense of lack of control over eating during the episode (e.g., a feeling that one cannot stop eating or control what and how much one is eating).

2. Recurrent inappropriate compensatory behavior in order to prevent weight gain, such as self-induced vomiting; misuse of laxatives, diuretics, enemas, or other medications; fasting or excessive exercise.

3. The binge eating and inappropriate compensatory behaviors occur, on average, at least twice a week for 3 months.

4. The disturbance does not occur exclusively during episodes of anorexia nervosa. Bulimia nervosa is also subdivided into two categories: purging type, in which the person regularly compensates for binging by purging; and nonpurging type, in which the person fasts or exercises excessively but does not purge.

This admittedly arbitrary quantification excludes many people who obviously have disordered eating habits—who may indeed be critically ill—but who fail to meet the criteria for one of the two full-fledged eating disorder diagnoses. This includes, for example, a female who meets all the criteria for anorexia nervosa except that she still menstruates, or a person who meets all the criteria for bulimia nervosa except that he or she has binged and purged for less than three months. A variety of harmful eating practices falls into a catchall nondiagnosis category in the *DSM-IV*, Eating Disorder Not Otherwise Specified, or EDNOS.

The EDNOS category is the focus of most of the controversy over the definition of eating disorders, because it is the official dividing line between normal and abnormal behavior. This is not merely an academic distinction. People who fall in the EDNOS nondiagnosis category are less likely to qualify for medical insurance coverage or disability benefits, and their disorders are less likely to get researchers' attention. As Columbia associate professor of clinical psychiatry Michael First argues, "If you feel that there's a homogeneous group of patients in there for which there's a treatment, the fact that it's called Not Otherwise Specified really obscures it, hindering treatment, hindering research."

It takes compelling data to convince clinicians that a mental illness deserves its own definition. This appears to be the case for one EDNOS, binge-eating disorder, or BED. A person with BED binges at least two times a week, but unlike a person with bulimia nervosa, does not purge, fast, or excessively exercise. Not surprisingly, BED is associated with severe obesity. In the *DSM-IV*, BED is singled out for "provisional diagnostic" status in the EDNOS category, a preliminary step to full diagnosis pending further research. In February 2007, a team of Harvard Medical School researchers reported that binge-eating disorder is actually four times more common and tends to persist longer than anorexia and bulimia; this surprising finding supports the promotion of BED to full eating disorder diagnosis status in the fifth revision of the *DSM*, due in 2011.

The difficulty of precisely defining eating disorders fuels ongoing debate over their true incidence and over the hypocrisy of simultaneously pathologizing and idolizing thinness in contemporary America. *Eating Disorders: Opposing Viewpoints* examines these and other issues through the opinions and analyses of experts including physicians, sociologists, people with eating disorders, and others in the following chapters: Are Eating Disorders a Serious Problem? What Causes Eating Disorders? What Role Does the Internet Play in Eating Disorders? How Should Eating Disorders Be Treated? The diverse views presented in this book illustrate the complexity of disorders that are even more powerful than the fundamental need to eat.

CHAPTER 1

Are Eating Disorders a Serious Problem?

Chapter Preface

Estimates of the incidence of eating disorders (EDs) vary widely. Many ED professionals believe shame and guilt over fasting, binging, and purging behaviors, and strong reluctance to give up those behaviors, keep a significant number of people with EDs from identifying themselves or seeking treatment. Experts therefore gather information on known sufferers—usually inpatients in eating disorder treatment facilities or research study participants—and extrapolate these findings to the general population. On this basis, according to Susan Ice of the Renfrew Center and the *Journal of the American Academy of Child and Adolescent Psychiatry*, 0.5 to 3.7 percent of females suffer from anorexia nervosa, 1.1 to 4.2 percent of females suffer from bulimia nervosa, and 2 to 5 percent of males and females suffer from binge-eating disorder. Most cases of anorexia emerge during adolescence, and certain groups—athletes and dancers of both sexes, for example—are considered especially vulnerable. Anorexia nervosa is widely cited as the most dangerous ED, with a mortality rate of up to 20 percent, the highest of any mental illness.

Certainly the public, most familiar with news and shocking images of emaciated young women, assumes anorexia nervosa is the most common ED. In February 2007, however, the first national survey on eating disorders challenged this assumption with data that show binge-eating disorder, not the better-known anorexia nervosa or bulimia nervosa, is the most common eating disorder. The National Comorbidity Survey Replication (NCS-R) is a two-year survey of more than nine thousand people across the country, led by James I. Hudson, director of the Psychiatric Epidemiology Research Program at McLean Hospital and professor of psychiatry at Harvard Medical School. In the NCS-R, 0.9 percent of women and 0.3 percent of men reported having anorexia nervosa at some point in their lives; 1.5 percent of women and 0.5 percent of men reported having bulimia nervosa. A surprising 3.5 percent of women and 2 percent of men reported having binge-eating disorder, roughly four times more than are afflicted with anorexia.

The study also draws surprising conclusions about the duration of eating disorders. According to survey respondents, the average duration of anorexia is 1.7 years, bulimia 8.3 years, and binge-eating disorder 8.1 years. This contradicts the belief that anorexia is often chronic, and suggests that binge-eating disorder, which involves uncontrolled eating without purging and persists much longer, is not getting enough attention.

Calling binge-eating disorder a "major public health burden," Hudson calls for increased prevention and treatment programs: "Everybody knows about anorexia and bulimia; however, binge-eating disorder affects more people, is often associated with severe obesity, and tends to persist longer. . . . The consequences of binge-eating disorder can be serious—including obesity, diabetes, heart disease, high blood pressure, and stroke. It is imperative that health experts take notice of these findings." The contributors to the following chapter debate the role of binge-eating disorder on rates of obesity in the United States, whether eating disorders are on the rise, and whether EDs in general pose a serious public health threat.

> "If we do not begin widespread, well-researched, effective eating disorder prevention programs ... the costs to our society and to our health care system will be devastating."

Eating Disorders Are a Growing Public Health Threat

Eating Disorders Coalition for Research, Policy & Action

The Eating Disorders Coalition for Research, Policy & Action (EDC), founded in 2000 and based in Washington, D.C., is an association of ten professional, medical research, and family foundation groups that advocates the expansion of research programs and insurance coverage for eating disorders as a public health priority. In the following viewpoint, the EDC argues that incidence of eating disorders is growing among all demographic groups; that the physical, psychological, and social costs of eating disorders are severe; and that existing prevention and treatment programs are inadequate.

Eating Disorders Coalition for Research, Policy & Action, testimony at the Hearing on Women's Health before the U.S. Senate Health, Education, Labor, and Pensions Committee, Subcommittee on Public Health, on the "Promoting Healthy Eating Behaviors in Youth Act of 2002 as Part of a Women's Omnibus Health Bill," 107th Cong., 2nd sess., April 25, 2002. Reproduced by permission.

As you read, consider the following questions:

1. According to the EDC, what is the incidence of eating disorders in the United States?
2. What does the author estimate as the mortality rate of anorexia?
3. How do insurance companies contribute to the high death rate of eating disorders, according to the EDC?

E ating disorders, though not uncommon, especially among women, continue to go unrecognized as an important health priority, and are often overlooked entirely in national health campaigns. . . . Until Congress addresses eating disorders through research, treatment and prevention more young people will suffer and die unnecessarily. [Legislation] promoting healthy eating as a way to prevent eating disorders and other health problems is an important step in recognizing eating disorders as a public health threat in need of policy attention.

Eating Disorders as a Public Health Threat

Eating disorders are a growing public health threat with an estimated 8 million Americans suffering from eating disorders. Eating disorders cut across race, color, gender and socioeconomic categories. No one is immune. Eating disorders wreak havoc on a person's psyche and body. They are commonly associated with substantial psychological problems, including depression, substance abuse, and all too frequently with suicide. They also can lead to major medical complications, including cardiac arrhythmia, cognitive impairment, osteoporosis, infertility, and most seriously death. Anorexia nervosa has the highest mortality rate of all the psychiatric disorders. A young woman with anorexia is 12 times more likely to die than other women her age without anorexia. The frequency of suicide is 75 times greater than expected in young women without eating disorders.

The Need for Access to Care

The challenges for people with eating disorders accessing appropriate treatment have created a lethal situation. We receive calls practically every week from those suffering from eating disorders, their families or friends seeking help accessing treatment. Just this week we received a call about a 15-year-old girl in the hospital with severe anorexia weighing only 55 pounds and being fed through tubes—whose health insurance company refused her coverage because anorexia is a mental disorder not a physical disease. Last week we received a call from a young woman in a residential treatment center who was panic stricken as she was told that her insurance company would not pay for her treatment. In her darkest hour, when she is already feeling defeated and unworthy, she is forced to fight for the care she so desperately needs. The week prior to this we received two such calls.

Health insurance companies contribute to the high death rate by either denying care or limiting the number of days they will reimburse for treatment. Research shows that eating disorders can be successfully overcome with adequate and appropriate treatment. Yet such treatments are typically extensive and long-term. The practice of insurance companies routinely limiting the number of days they will reimburse forces doctors to discharge patients with anorexia nervosa too early. Although patients with eating disorders typically require more than 6 weeks of inpatient therapy, hospitalization or residential treatment for proper recovery, insurance companies offer an average of 10–15 days a year. Typically, insurers completely ignore the standards of care for eating disorders established by the American Psychiatric Association and published in the *APA Journal* in 2000.

According to a survey of eating disorder specialists conducted in conjunction with ANAD [the National Association of Anorexia Nervosa and Associated Disorders], 100% said

An Inadequate Government Response to a Growing Health Problem

There is less money available for research on eating disorders than there is for any other known health condition. Research into causes and treatments for eating disorders is conducted by several universities and government institutions, but the overwhelming majority of this research is funded and conducted by the National Institute of Mental Health [NIMH]. The most recent year for which reliable figures are available is 2003 during which the NIMH spent 1.5 percent of its annual research budget on eating disorders research—this 1.5 percent equals a total of about $20.1 million. That sounds like a lot of money, but is actually less than the total amount spent for research on any other condition handled by the NIMH. When you take prevalence into account, 1.5 percent of the NIMH budget turns out to be very little money indeed. Here's why—we know how many people are afflicted with each of the different conditions researched by the NIMH, and we know how much money is spent on researching these conditions—so it's a simple task to find out how much money is spent by the NIMH *per case* for each of the conditions that they research: total research funds divided by prevalence equals per case funds. . . .

Illness	Per Case Research Funds
Schizophrenia	$141.77
Bipolar Disorder	$ 37.78
Autism	$ 34.07
Major Depression	$11.20
Eating Disorders	$ 00.74

Chris Kraatz, Radical Recovery: A Manifesto of Eating Disorder Pride. *Lanham, MD: University Press of America, 2006.*

that their patients are suffering relapses as a consequence of such managed care coverage limits. And virtually all specialists believed that patients with anorexia are placed in life-threatening situations because their health insurance policies mandate early discharge.

Passing [a] mental health parity bill for those with eating disorders is a matter of life and death. The longer Congress waits the more young people we will lose. We urge Congress to pass this bill with haste.

Important Role of Prevention

In addition to pushing for treatment for those currently suffering from eating disorders it is equally important to offer prevention programs for youth. Primary efforts are designed to prevent the occurrence of eating disorders before they begin by promoting healthy development.

Experts on optimal prevention programs for eating disorders conclude that successful programs are designed to promote healthy development, thus are multidimensional and comprehensive. Successful curricula include not only information about nutritional content but also information about responding to hunger and satiety, positive body image development, positive self-esteem development, and learning life skills, such as stress management, communication skills, problem solving and decision-making skills. Successful interventions are tailored to the developmental and cultural needs of the target population and include family, school and community involvement.

Basic Principles for the Prevention of Eating Disorders

Eating disorder prevention experts Margo Maine, Ph.D., and Michael Levine, Ph.D., outline a number of important principles for prevention efforts as outlined here.

1. Given that eating disorders are serious and complex problems we need to avoid thinking of them in simplis-

tic terms, like "anorexia is just a plea for attention," or "bulimia is just an addiction to food." Eating disorders arise from a variety of physical, emotional, social, and familial issues, all of which need to be addressed for effective prevention and treatment.

2. The objectification and other forms of mistreatment of women by others contribute directly to two underlying features of an eating disorder: obsession with appearance and shame about one's body.

3. Eating disorders are not just a "woman's problem" or "something for the girls." Males who are preoccupied with shape and weight can also develop eating disorders as well as dangerous shape control practices like steroid use.

4. Prevention efforts will fail, or worse, inadvertently encourage disordered eating, if they concentrate solely on warning the public about the signs, symptoms, and dangers of eating disorders. Effective prevention programs must also address:

   • Our cultural obsession with slenderness as a physical, psychological, and moral issue.

   • The roles of men and women in our society.

   • The development of people's self-esteem and self-respect in a variety of areas (school, work, community service, hobbies) that transcend physical appearance.

5. Whenever possible, prevention programs for schools, community organizations, etc., should be coordinated with opportunities for participants to speak confidentially with a trained professional with expertise in the field of eating disorders, and, when appropriate, receive referrals to sources of competent, specialized care.

Promoting a Healthy Environment for Youth

In addition to inoculating the individual from developing disordered eating, effective prevention efforts should also create positive environments for youth in which they may flourish. Such environments would emphasize the value of each child, promote a sense of self-efficacy and confidence, be free from harassment and violence, respond appropriately to teasing and bullying, separate a child's worth from beauty and body weight, offer nutritional and tasty food options, offer opportunities for exercise and play, encourage youth to value their uniqueness and the uniqueness of others, and other factors that promote the healthy development of youth.

Efforts designed to promote healthy eating must be done in such a way as to not inadvertently create new problems. Focusing on body weight and urging youth to be thin has not helped reduce the prevalence of overweight. Instead it has resulted in a host of new health problems such as widespread body dissatisfaction, poor body image, low self-esteem, pathogenic weight control practices, and eating disorders. Therefore, effective interventions for promoting healthy eating with youth should promote a healthy lifestyle and not promote unhealthy weight management techniques.

The Dire Need for Prevention Research Dollars

If we do not begin widespread, well-researched, effective eating disorder prevention programs to foster healthy eating habits in youth, the costs to our society and to our health care system will be devastating. As many as 5–10% of people with anorexia nervosa or bulimia nervosa will die prematurely— many struck down in the prime of their lives. Even those who recover suffer needlessly, impairing their intellectual, academic, vocational, economic, social, emotional and personal functioning. Furthermore, countless women of all ages and increasing numbers of men also suffer from sub-clinical eating disorders, demonstrating some, but not all, of the symptoms of eating disorders. As they are unlikely to receive treatment, their compromised nutritional intake can lead to serious health problems such as cardiac irregularities, chronic gastrointestinal disorders, infertility, osteoporosis, as well as severe anxiety and mood fluctuations.

The lack of substantial funding for prevention-oriented research is one of the greatest problems contributing to the ongoing increase in eating disorders and related conditions. The research done to date has begun to differentiate effective prevention approaches from ineffective ones. We desperately need more funding to build on this body of knowledge and begin to eradicate these life-destroying illnesses.

| "*Exaggerated claims about the extent of eating disorders, born of over-zealous diagnoses, risk fanning the flames of food distress.*"

The Problem of Eating Disorders Is Exaggerated

Malcolm Evans

In the following viewpoint, sociologist Malcolm Evans disputes claims that eating disorders affect 30 to 50 percent of women at some point in their lives. Not only are such figures exaggerated, Evans claims, but pathologizing general or low-level anxieties over dieting and body image makes it more likely that people will identify themselves as diseased, and thus victims of medical conditions they have no control over. He blames the research community as well as the media for pushing the definition of eating disorders beyond the only legitimate conditions, anorexia and bulimia. Malcolm Evans is the founder and secretary of the UK-based charitable organization The Weight Foundation, which researches dieting and problem eating.

As you read, consider the following questions:

1. When were anorexia and bulimia recognized as medical disorders, according to the author?
2. What does Evans say distinguishes binge-eating disorder from simple overeating?
3. According to Evans, why is it harder to treat obsessions with weight if the condition is categorized as a disease rather than a habit?

There is a thin line in any awareness campaign between shouting too loudly and shouting the wrong things.

With the West seemingly gripped in general by a growing obesity crisis and with nervous parents constantly vigilant for signs of eating disorders in their children, there is greater confusion than ever before surrounding the entire subject of food and eating.

But whilst serious eating disorders are unequivocally horrible and frequently life-threatening, pushing too many problem eaters and hardcore dieters too hastily towards definitive eating disorder status may be causing harm.

Sending out the wrong cries for help can have limiting abilities for self-help and recovery.

Exaggerated claims about the extent of eating disorders, born of over-zealous diagnoses, risk fanning the flames of food distress.

One sees figures being bandied about that 30–50% of women will experience an eating disorder at some stage within their lifetime.

This author does not for one minute believe that up to half of women will suffer an eating disorder. But what isolated individuals believe matters not at all; if people expect themselves to be at risk in such contexts, then risk automatically increases and if that risk is quasi-medical, it assumes a certain inevitability.

Anorexia: An Overblown Threat

A 2001 study by the University of British Columbia's Department of Psychology of *every American death for the most recently available five year period* showed only 724 people with anorexia as a causal factor—145 per year. Christina Hoff-Sommers, in her research for the book *Who Stole Feminism*, came up with a number below half that. In a presentation to the International Congress of Psychology, one expert (Dr. Paul Hewitt) estimated a death rate for anorexia of 6.6 per 100,000 deaths. Even if you assume that sufferers outnumber deaths by a few orders of magnitude, it would still seem that all objective evidence shows the health impact on Americans from anorexia is statistically nil. Now, I know that doesn't make for very good shock journalism, but it doesn't change the uncomfortable fact that it's true.

Anthony Citrano, "The Haunting Myth of American Anorexia,"
The Cosmic Tap, April 2, 2006. www.cosmictap.com.

Pathologizing on a Grand Scale

This is pathologizing on a grand scale—the categorization of problems or conditions into diseases. Once issues have become concretized like this, the focus of remedy changes. It goes from being voluntary habit change to becoming treatment only by expert third parties.

In fact, the subject deserves another big word—somatization. This is how individuals experience distress as symptoms. It is a process nowhere near as set in stone as one might think. For instance, there is such a stigma attaching to any form of mental illness in some Eastern cultures that people suffering from what would immediately be recognized in the West as depression may characterize their suffering as stomach pains.

It is equally clear that someone around whom the net of "disorder" is cast may feel herself trapped much more inescapably than another person who is advised to work through certain lifestyle issues.

Beyond this there is a credibility issue. It is incredibly easy to be condemned as reactionary or uncaring when criticizing the voices of any minority. However, history shows that any overstatement or inaccuracy risks damaging the core cause. One only needs to look back at the Gay Rights movement of the 1970's and 1980's to remember how perhaps over-enthusiastic estimates of the population's gay percentage led to opponents shifting the field of argument. With this one area of accuracy challenged, the otherwise overpowering case for equality and decency was less clearly advanced.

In a completely different context, the campaign to address the reported plight of Vietnam Veterans in the post-war civilian U.S. was blighted by subsequent highly-credible studies which undermined the reported numbers of individuals concerned, if not the problem issues themselves.

Moving back to eating disorders, definitions until quite recently have generally comprised Anorexia and Bulimia. Whilst there are various earlier references to self-starvation, particularly amongst young women, going back in to classical antiquity, it was not until the latter part of the 19th Century that a medical typology of Anorexia was constructed. Bulimia was first formally noted in 1979.

The research community has for some time been exploring 'Binge Eating Disorder' to capture the notion of repeated and out of control overeating. BED as a firmer concept is now ring-fenced with a considerable array of necessary behaviors, anxieties and obsessions to differentiate it from lesser overeating.

The Media Leads an Eating Disorders Bandwagon

Despite the cautious progress of researchers in testing the boundaries, there is a less sophisticated eating disorders bandwagon creating a disruptive momentum. As ever in all matters eating problem related, the media is an avid recipient, presenter and sometimes creator of sensationalism . . . 30 ft [9 m] slithers become 100 ft [30 m] plunges; an unease around eating becomes a panic. . . .

Individual issues of self-image anxieties, overeating, continual dieting and obesity worries are being conflated into broad ranging and quasi-medical identities.

This is not in any way to downplay the dangers and distress caused by full-blown eating disorders, serious binge eating included (nor to point the finger in any way at the many responsible and research-driven advocacy groups).

But people can exercise far more control over what is personal and cultural than they can over what is seen as endemic and medical. Wherever the serious debate finally settles with some certainty in these areas, it is absolutely clear that there is too much hype seeping in at present.

The more that people are over-hastily pushed down the road of disease labeling, the lower their chances of establishing and maintaining a natural and relaxed relationship with food. Some eating disorder zealots—and sensationalist reporters—are doing a disservice to both the sufferers of major conditions and also those experiencing other unpleasant eating issues.

| "White women make up 90% of people who suffer from eating disorders."

Eating Disorders Primarily Affect White Western Women

Anne Iverson

In the following viewpoint, Anne Iverson contends that the conventional view of eating disorders as disproportionately affecting young white Western women is correct. Black women, Iverson finds, are less susceptible to eating disorders because they value qualities such as attitude and style over body type and size, identify less with images of white, thin celebrities and fashion models; and may consciously resist dominant thin standards of beauty to gain a sense of control in a culture that devalues African Americans socially and economically. Anne Iverson's senior seminar research, from which this article is excerpted, was named best women's studies senior thesis at Kansas University in 2005.

As you read, consider the following questions:

1. How do black women's and white women's standards of beauty differ, according to Iverson?

Anne Iverson, "Mind Over Matter: Race, Body Image, and Eating Disorders," senior thesis, Women's Studies Senior Seminar, University of Kansas, Women's Studies Department, May 10, 2005. www.womensstudies.ku.edu/senior_seminar/anne_iverson _paper.doc. Copyright © 2005 by the University of Kansas. Reproduced by permission of the author.

2. How are male expectations of physical appearance perceived differently by black and white women, in Iverson's findings?

3. What percentage of people who suffer from eating disorders are white women, according to the author?

The implications of race in studies about anorexia and bulimia have only begun to emerge in the last ten years. While available studies are often helpful in explaining the difference between levels of eating disorders among White and Black women in the United States, many are less successful in explaining *why* this is the case.

By examining eating disorders in the context of race, we can further understand why some people are more affected than others and what causes contribute to the higher level of eating disorders we have seen in the last 20 years. Deeper understanding of this issue can also improve how the discourse on eating disorders affects who receives attention and treatment and who does not. . . .

How are beauty ideals and eating disorders related? Why do white women have more eating disorders than black women in the United States? Do women have any agency regarding disordered eating? The factors that contribute to who suffers from eating disorders are complex, interconnected, and vary greatly depending on personal histories and backgrounds. As this paper will illustrate, White women are more likely to suffer from anorexia and bulimia than Black women for a variety of reasons, including personal, societal, and cultural expectations. . . .

Beauty Ideals

Recent studies propose that White women and Black women have different concepts of what makes women attractive. White adolescent girls tend to describe their ideal in terms of a uniform set of physical attributes encapsulated in the word "perfect." There seems to be one body figure above all others, which is rationally unattainable but should be strived for anyway because the closer a girl can come to this figure, the more perfect she is.

For Black adolescent girls, however, the story is much different. They tend to de-emphasize external beauty, instead describing their ideal girl in terms of personality traits, style, attitude, and ability to project a sense of pride and confidence. Also, Black girls tend to be more flexible than their white counterparts in their concepts of beauty, and express greater satisfaction with their body shape. Along with this flexibility, Black female participants in a focus group on race and body image reported that style and grooming is significantly more important than body regulation and manipulation to their Black peers. One theme that appeared among participants was that trust and attitude is more important than physical appearance when determining what is beautiful for Black women.

These very different attitudes about how to elevate oneself to the ideal standard of beauty speaks to the discrepancy of eating disorder prevalence between Black and White women. As White women are more focused on body size and manipulation while Black women are focused on outward style and attitude, it follows that White women would suffer from eating disorders at a much higher level.

Gendered Expectations

One of the initial reasons many women weight-watch is the desire to be attractive to potential sexual partners. While it is true that women often gauge their own attractiveness in comparison to other women, the ultimate objective appears to be attractiveness toward men. Given this, it logically follows that women's perceptions of male expectations play a role in how they view themselves.

Interestingly, White and Black women have different perceptions of these expectations. According to [Kushal A.] Patel & [James J.] Gray, African American women accurately estimate the level of thinness preferred by African American men. White women, on the other hand, show a greater difference between the body shapes guessed to be most attractive to the opposite sex and what members of the opposite sex actually preferred. While Black women seem to know exactly how their bodies must look in order to be attractive to men, White women assume that men want them to be thinner than the men actually desire.

Moreover, there is an analogous difference between Black and White women regarding their ideal and current figure perceptions. Although African American women experience variance between their ideal and current figure perceptions, these discrepancies are not as large as those for Caucasian women, suggesting that Black women are less dissatisfied with their bodies. Thus, women's perceptions of what they are expected to look like affects how attractive they consider themselves.

Media Influences

A further explanation for Black women's more positive body images is the greater proportion of positive Black female body images in the media. The majority of images in mainstream media that depict sexualized White women show very thin and fashion-model type bodies that do not reflect the actual physical experience of White women. This is also true to an extent for Black women; however, it is more common for sexualized images of Black women to include fuller bodies and more generous standards for size and weight.

Despite the healthier images of Black women in mainstream media, Black women as a whole are underrepresented. Most of the images women see everyday are of thin, white women who have been airbrushed into perfection. If these are

Studies Confirm Prevalence of Eating Disorders Among White Females

Consistent with epidemiological studies in North America, Europe, and Australia, our [July 2003 study] results suggest that all eating disorders are relatively uncommon and that anorexia nervosa is the least common, while binge eating disorder is the most common of the three eating disorders. The prevalence and ages of onset of anorexia nervosa and bulimia nervosa observed in our sample of white women were well within the ranges reported in other studies of white women in the United States and Canada. For example, the number of white women with anorexia nervosa and bulimia nervosa observed in this study (15 and 23 of about 1,000 women, respectively) was comparable to the lifetime prevalence rates (1.4% and 2.5%) in a community sample of similar ages recruited in Oregon. Research has shown that late adolescence is the period of greatest risk for the onset of anorexia nervosa and bulimia nervosa and that onset after age 21 is rare. Nevertheless, in our sample of more than 1,000 black women (ages 19–24), no case of anorexia nervosa was detected, and the odds of detecting bulimia nervosa were six-fold greater for white women than for black women.

Ruth H. Striegel-Moore et al.,
"Eating Disorders in White and Black Women,"
American Journal of Psychiatry, *July 2003, pp. 1326–31.*

the images both White and Black women see, how do they affect each race? Of course, media plays a role in internalization of social standards of appearance, regardless of ethnic group. Interestingly, [Cynthia M.] Frisby points out that African-American women are affected by images of other black women in the media much more than they are affected by images of white women. She proposes that black women do not compare themselves to white women in the media, but do compare themselves to similar black women. . . .

Socioeconomics

Women who have a higher socioeconomic status are commonly thought to be more susceptible to eating disorders. A possible explanation for this is that many of the very thin women seen in daily life in the United States are white and appear to be wealthy. When researchers try to study this proposition, however, this conclusion is not so easily drawn.

One theory on the correlation between disordered eating and socioeconomic status is that concerns about dieting and weight have shifted from the upper class into mainstream consciousness. Indeed, it was once thought that women of higher socioeconomic status had more intense attitudes about thinness, but now the concern about dieting and weight has become so widespread in Western culture that a moderate level of concern is normative. Moreover, studies show that when Black women adopt more values from the predominant White culture, they report greater pressures to diet and they exhibit more problematic eating behavior. . . .

Cultural Explanations

Viewing the causes of eating disorders in the context of race provides a new set of variables that can affect how likely someone is to develop anorexia or bulimia. Unfortunately, the cultural implications have not been fully studied by researchers, and there is very little writing about it even in feminist works. Indeed, it seems that how Black women relate to each other within their own ethnicity and to the pressure of society at large influences how likely they are to have an eating disorder.

Women experience overwhelming societal pressures to look and behave a certain way when comparing and contrasting themselves with other women. What is seen as attractive in one person is what is desirable in another. Does race make a difference in the kinds of pressures women face to conform?

The research that does include race and other variables in its analysis suggests that Black women relate to one another differently than White women in terms of body image ideals. Black women may be less likely to acquire eating disorders due to differences in the cultural construction of femininity in Black communities. The difference seems to be that Black women who live in Black communities focus less on body type and size, and instead look at beauty in terms of style, personality, pride, and how a woman carries herself in general. One study that asked women of color exactly why they think Black women have fewer eating disorders concluded that an Afro centric aesthetic that is based on concepts of uniqueness and harmony in diversity, and on unity of mind, body, and spirit could create a more positive environment that sends fewer messages to young women that tell them they are not physically acceptable.

In a nationwide study, [Thomas F.] Cash & [Patricia E.] Henry propose that one reason African American women show more body satisfaction, less overweight concern, and more favorable body image is because of African American culture's broader latitude of acceptance concerning women's body size. Since much of the policing of body size comes from other women, a more accepting environment among Black women could significantly reduce the desire to be thin.

Acculturation

If Black women feel safe and confident within their own ethnic communities, the same cannot be said for the women assimilating into the dominant White society. As Black women slowly but surely move higher in job markets and find themselves side by side with weight-conscious White culture, they develop more awareness and sensitivity to these expectations of thinness.

According to [Laura S.] Abrams and [Colleen Cook] Stormer in 2002, African American girls who had more ethnically diverse peer groups had higher awareness of media messages about ideal body types, and internalized these messages more than African American girls with more homogenous ethnic peer groups. This indicates that when surrounded with African American friends, these girls felt protected against the influence of dominant standards of thinness. In contrast, the extent to which African American women identify with the dominant White culture may make them more vulnerable to body image distortions and eating disorders.

The apparent protection that comes from associating with other women of color lessens as Black women adopt values or behaviors that White culture emphasizes. Because thinness for White women is becoming more mainstream, Black women who seek to compete with others for jobs and social status face the same pressures.

Resistance

Finally, one of the most important explanations for the lower prevalence rate of eating disorders in Black women is the notion that these women use their agency over their bodies to resist a culture telling them they are inferior in a variety of ways. White culture has historically placed Black women on the bottom of the socioeconomic scale in the United States, and many Black women feel that resistance is needed to counteract oppressive, harmful messages from a society that devalues black looks and culture. . . .

Black women's cultural resistance to mainstream beauty ideals, differences in the cultural construction of the feminine gender role, and their need to deny physical and psychological vulnerability may help to explain why they have fewer eating disorders than their White counterparts. Instead of adjusting to ideals of thinness that become another layer atop numerous others that position Black women as worth less than other people in American society, these women use their bodies to promote self-determination.

Though economic success often necessitates accommodating dominant white, middle-class aesthetic and cultural values, women of color use their embodied ethnicity as a source of strength. Their development of strong self-valuations and alternative standards of appearance and character may be more liberating than mainstream ideals (the "perfect" woman). Also, supportive communities may help protect them from harmful psychological messages. In summary, Black women may develop a strong positive self-valuation and an alternative beauty aesthetic to resist societal stigmatization.

Prevailing assumptions lend themselves to the idea that all ethnicities are included in the discourse surrounding eating disorders, when in fact mostly white women suffer from anorexia and bulimia. Although White women make up 90% of people who suffer from eating disorders, Black women should not be ignored in the discussion of body image. By including Black women's voices in research on the issue, we can come to know more about how societal messages, family structures, and personal psychology affect disordered eating.

| *"Black women, Latina women, they all feel the need to be thin to fit in."*

Eating Disorders Are a Growing Problem Among Minority Women

Denise Brodey

The prevalence of anorexia, bulimia, and binge-eating disorder is significant and growing among African American, Asian, and Hispanic women, according to health and fitness writer Denise Brodey. In the following viewpoint, Brodey maintains that medical professionals too often overlook signs of eating disorders in minority women, based on outdated assumptions that only young white women are susceptible. She cites research indicating, on the contrary, that black female college students are even more likely to report binge eating, fasting, and laxative abuse than white female students, though they are less likely to seek treatment. Denise Brodey is editor in chief of Fitness *magazine and the author of a book about parenting special-needs children,* The Elephant in the Playroom.

As you read, consider the following questions:

1. According to Brodey, why were black women traditionally less vulnerable to eating disorders than their white peers?

2. What factors contribute to the increase in eating disorders in minority women, according to the author?

3. Why are African American women less likely to seek treatment for eating disorders, in Brodey's view?

As a teenager, Nickona Knuckles regularly binged on food and then vomited to keep her weight down.

Ms. Knuckles, who is African-American, recalled that at the time she had no idea of the devastating health effects of bulimia, nor did she care. She was one of nine black students in a high school of 3,000 and was struggling simply to be accepted.

"When it came to body image, my perception of beauty was based on my white peers and images of white celebrities in the media," Ms. Knuckles, now 34, said in an interview at her home in Phoenix. "I didn't want to be white but it was very difficult to be comfortable with who I was."

Her parents, concerned about her eating problem, took her to an outpatient treatment program in Mesa, Ariz.

But, Ms. Knuckles said, the program did not help her.

"The place was filled with white people and, to be honest, there was nobody who looked like me or could relate to me," she said. Eating disorders like bulimia and anorexia conjure images of affluent white teenage girls. And most studies of these disorders have focused on white patients.

In recent years, however, more blacks and other minorities have been seeking help from eating disorder clinics. "We're noticing a trend of more severe eating disorders among African-American girls," said Dr. Gayle Brooks, an African-American psychologist and vice president of clinical services at the Renfrew Center in Coconut Creek, Fla., an eating disorders treatment center.

Eating Disorders Increasingly Cross Color Lines

While it was once believed that anorexia, binge-eating and bulimia only affected white, middle- to upper-class, college-educated women, there are now reports of eating disorders among racial and ethnic minorities in the United States, according to a recent study in *Pediatrics*. . . .

"Eating disorders affect women (and men) of every age, race, socioeconomic background and sexual orientation," says [social worker Deborah] Taylor. "The specific nature of the most common eating problems, as well as risk and protective factors, may vary from group to group, but no population or culture is exempt.". . .

Minority and lower-income women do not fit the old profile, and stereotyped body images of minority women (e.g., the belief that most Asian-American women are petite and most African-American women are heavier) can still hinder detection of eating disorders by medical professionals.

Joanna Pompilio, "Crossing the Color Lines:
The Face of Eating Disorders in 2006,"
WashingtonWoman.com, February 2006.

Dr. Brooks said experts traditionally had thought that "anorexia and bulimia didn't happen to black, Asian or Hispanic women, that they were somehow immune."

In fact, she said, African-American women had in the past been less likely than white women to feel the same pressures to be thin.

"Curvy African-American women were celebrated," Dr. Brooks said. "These girls didn't experience anxiety and shame about their bodies. Being curvy or large was a source of pride within the African-American community."

Up to 4.2 percent of American women at some point in their lives suffer from bulimia, according to the National Institute of Mental Health. The disorder is characterized by binge eating and purging by vomiting, excessive exercise or laxative abuse. Anorexia nervosa, in which people starve themselves to extremely low weight, afflicts up to 3.7 percent of American women over their lifetimes.

No reliable numbers exist for how many minority women suffer from eating problems, but experts suspect that cases are increasing.

In a 2003 study, for example, published in the *American Journal of Psychiatry*, Dr. Ruth Striegel-Moore, professor and chairwoman of psychology at Wesleyan University, found that young black women were as likely as white women to report binge eating. In an earlier study, published in 2000 in *Archives of Family Medicine*, she found that black women were as likely as white women to report binge eating or vomiting and were more likely to report fasting and the abuse of laxatives or diuretics than their white peers.

One reason experts do not know how many minorities suffer from the disorders, Dr. Striegel-Moore said, is that minority women are less likely to seek treatment.

In her research, she found that of the 76 women who ever had an eating disorder, 16, or 28 percent, of the white women and 1, or 5 percent, of the black women reported having received treatment for an eating disorder.

"Minority women are not getting treated," Dr. Striegel-Moore said. "It's very clear from my studies that black American women do experience eating disorders, but doctors and therapists still operate under the assumption that they don't; therefore they aren't prepared to deal with them clinically."

News coverage of eating disorders is almost always focused on white patients, she said. Doctors may not be alert for the symptoms of eating disorders in minority women, and therefore may not ask the right questions or refer them for specialized treatment.

A Florida State University study lends support to this observation. The researchers showed fictional diaries of a 16-year-old girl to 150 people. When the diarist was identified as white, most people said the subject, called Mary, had an eating disorder. When she was identified as black, far fewer people identified her as having an eating disorder.

Minority women face other barriers to getting care, as well, Dr. Striegel-Moore said, including "lack of resources and insurance and not knowing who to contact."

Compounding the problem said Dr. Kevin Thompson, a professor of psychology at the University of South Florida, is that body dissatisfaction among African-American, Hispanic and Asian-American women "is catching up rapidly to that of white women."

In some cases, minority women believe that being thin will help them fit into mainstream white culture. "In the past 10 years, there has been a tremendous cultural shift: The image of the ideal body image is narrower," said Dr. Ira Sacker, an expert in eating disorders and founder of the Helping End Eating Disorders Foundation in New York. "Black women, Latina women, they all feel the need to be thin to fit in."

But Dr. Sacker said he now saw more minority women in his practice.

Dr. Stefanie Gilbert, assistant professor of psychology at Howard University in Washington [D.C.], said black women pictured in magazines often had body types similar to those of white models.

"These types also seem to be the ones who get the top jobs," Dr. Gilbert said.

Paradoxically, said Dr. Striegel-Moore, the increased pressure on minority women to be thin has stemmed in part from companies' efforts to increase diversity in their advertising, with images of thin, beautiful Asian-, Hispanic- and African-Americans joining those of whites.

But media images are not the only factors in the development of eating disorders. Studies show that being overstressed and overweight also puts women at risk, Dr. Striegel-Moore said. Eating disorders often begin in the early teenage years and carry into the 20's, although researchers have recently begun to document cases of middle-aged women developing the disorders.

Gradually, experts say, medical organizations and treatment programs are becoming more aware of eating disorders among minorities. The Renfrew Center, for example, has held lunches and special informational workshops for minority therapists.

Dr. Elena Rios, president and chief executive officer of the National Hispanic Medical Association, said, "Nutrition is on our radar, obesity is on our radar and now eating disorders are, too."

But experts say that African-American psychotherapists and other doctors who treat minorities need to be educated about the problem and they, in turn, need to reach out to their communities, Dr. Brooks said.

"An eating disorder is an illness," Dr. Brooks said. "There are treatments for it, but unless the medical community is trained to identify the illness in women of color, a lot of women suffering will not get treatment."

Ms. Knuckles, who began bingeing and purging when she was 12, might have benefited from such awareness and received effective treatment earlier.

"If I had been helped sooner I would have done a lot less damage to my body," she said.

"A significant proportion of obese persons have distress and dysfunction due to binge eating."

Eating Disorders Contribute to the Epidemic of Obesity in America

Susan Z. Yanovski

Medical researcher Susan Z. Yanovski argues in the following viewpoint that binge-eating disorder (BED) may be a significant risk factor for future weight gain, and that effectively treating BED may decrease the prevalence of severe obesity in the United States. Yanovski cites obesity-treatment studies that show participants who did not binge-eat maintained small but significant weight loss a year after treatment, but participants who continued to binge-eat either gained or did not lose weight. Susan Z. Yanovski is codirector of the Office of Obesity Research at the National Institute of Diabetes and Digestive and Kidney Diseases (NIDDK), a division of the National Institutes of Health, in Bethesda, Maryland.

As you read, consider the following questions:

1. What is the incidence of obesity in U.S. adults, according to Yanovski?

2. What is the estimated prevalence of binge-eating disorder (BED) among the severely obese treatment-seeking population, according to the author?

3. In the five-year study cited by Yanovski, what percentage of participants with BED were obese at the beginning of the study? at the end of the study?

Binge eating in the absence of compensatory behaviors was first described in the scientific literature more than four decades ago (Stunkard, 1959). Its modern rebirth as binge eating disorder (BED) occurred in 1992 and 1993, with a series of field studies conducted by [R.L.] Spitzer et al. (1992, 1993). Studies of obese individuals who sought treatment identified subgroups who experienced distress and dysfunction due to binge eating. It remains to be determined how these individuals differ from others with established eating disorders such as bulimia nervosa or from obese individuals who do not binge eat. Controversy existed in the early 1990s (Fairburn, Welch, & Hay, 1993) and still exists today (Stunkard, 2000) as to whether BED should be elevated to the position of a recognized psychiatric disorder in its own right, rather than as an example of an eating disorder not otherwise specified (EDNOS). During the last decade, there have been many studies on the etiology of BED, its risk factors, comorbidities, pathophysiology, and treatment. A MEDLINE search revealed more than 250 scientific papers related to the topic since 1995.

In 2002, the United States (and, indeed, the developed world) is experiencing an epidemic of obesity. The latest data indicate that more than 30% of U.S. adults are obese (body mass index [BMI] $\geq$ 30 kg/m^2), compared with 23% in 1988–1994 (Flegal, Carroll, Ogden, & Johnson, 2002). Obesity among children and adolescents is also increasing (Ogden,

Flegal, Carroll, & Johnson, 2002). With this rise in prevalence comes an increase in obesity-related diseases, such as Type 2 diabetes. Because it is unlikely that a major genetic shift has occurred over the past two decades, it is likely that our "toxic" environment, in combination with a genetic predisposition to energy efficiency, is contributing to the obesity epidemic (Wadden, Brownell, & Foster, 2002). Most obese people do not have BED. Prevalence estimates range from less than 2% in community studies to more than 25% in severely obese treatment-seeking populations (Yanovski, 1999). Using rigorous interview methodology for diagnosis decreases the prevalence, but it is clear that a significant proportion of obese persons have distress and dysfunction due to binge eating. Of particular concern is the reported association between binge eating and severe or extreme obesity (BMI ≥ 40; de Zwaan, 2001). The proportion of persons with extreme obesity is increasing even faster than the proportion of persons with lesser degrees of obesity (Freedman, Khan, Serdula, Galuska, & Dietz, 2002).

What do we know about the efficacy of weight loss treatments in patients with BED? Some studies show less weight loss, more rapid weight regain, or more attrition from treatment for those with BED (Sherwood, Jeffery, & Wing, 1999; Yanovski, Gormally, Lesser, Gwirtsman, & Yanovski, 1994), whereas others do not (Gladis et al., 1998). However, a significant portion of subjects with BED do at least as well in obesity treatment as those without an eating disorder. The coexistence of an affective disorder is a mediating factor (Sherwood et al., 1999). Consequently, characterizing individuals who meet criteria for BED by comorbid psychiatric conditions may be helpful in predicting response to treatment. Weight loss medications, although not well studied, have a similar effect in individuals with and without BED (Alger, Malone, Cerulli, Fein, & Howard, 1999). Additional studies of medications that may both induce weight loss and treat the underlying affective

Genetic Links Between Binge Eating Disorder and Obesity

Eating disorders and disturbed eating patterns are often associated with obesity. Aberrant eating behaviors that result in an imbalance between energy intake and energy expenditure not only contribute to excess weight gain but may also be associated with psychological distress. Although research has been inconsistent regarding whether obesity leads to disturbances in eating or disordered eating is a risk factor for the development of obesity, many obese individuals presenting for weight loss treatment report non-normative eating patterns. . . .

Even within the population meeting criteria for an eating disorder based on behavioral variables, there may be differences in outcome based on factors not previously considered, such as genetic variation. For example, polymorphisms of the melanocortin 4 (MC4) receptor have been identified in one study as being associated with binge eating. In that same population, a preliminary analysis found that patients with binge eating disorder [BED] who had an MC4 receptor polymorphism had less robust weight loss in response to bariatic surgery than patients with BED who did not have an MC4 receptor variant. Another preliminary study found decreased dopamine D2 receptor availability, as measured by positron emission tomography scanning, in obese individuals relative to normal-weight controls, suggesting a potential role for alterations in dopaminergic circuits as either a cause or a consequence of obesity.

Marian Tanofsky-Kraff and Susan Z. Yanovski,
"Eating Disorder or Disordered Eating?
Non-Normative Eating Patterns in Obese Individuals,"
Obesity Research, *vol. 12, 2004, pp. 1361–66.*

disorder, such as topiramate (Shapira, Goldsmith, & McElroy, 2000) and bupropion, are needed. Surprisingly, one small study that tested the efficacy of the anorectic dexfenfluramine in BED found that the drug led to decreases in binge eating without concomitant weight loss (Stunkard, Berkowitz, Tanrikut, Reiss, & Young, 1996). Bariatric surgery is increasingly used as a treatment for severe obesity. A substantial percentage of patients presenting for bariatric surgery meet criteria for BED (Hsu et al., 2002). It is possible that some surgical procedures (e.g., gastric bypass, which causes dumping with increased sweet consumption) may be superior to others, such as restrictive procedures, in severely obese BED patients. Further study in this area is also warranted.

Even among individuals who are not obese, BED may be an important risk factor for future weight gain. Community studies show that most individuals who meet criteria for BED are not obese, and almost one half are not even overweight (Fairburn, Cooper, Doll, Norman, & O'Connor, 2000; Spitzer et al., 1992, 1993; Yanovski, 1999). Binge eating precedes dieting in about one-half of BED individuals and may precede the development of obesity (Dingemans, Bruna, & van Furth, 2002). In a longitudinal community study, participants with BED gained an average of 4.2 ± 9.8 kg [9.3 ± 21.6 lb] over a 5-year period and the proportion of individuals who met criteria for obesity increased from 22% at baseline to 39% 5 years later (Fairburn et al., 2000). These data demonstrate that interventions for BED individuals who are not yet overweight may prevent inappropriate weight gain. Similarly, effective treatment for binge eating would decrease the prevalence of more severe obesity.

What evidence exists to test this hypothesis? Psychotherapy for BED, with either interpersonal psychotherapy (IPT) or cognitive-behavioral therapy (CBT), in the absence of weight loss treatment leads to a decrease in eating disorders symptoms but causes little weight loss (de Zwaan, 2001). However,

[D.E.] Wilfley et al. (2002) compared IPT with CBT and found that subjects who abstained from binge eating had small, but significant, reductions in BMI at both the end of treatment and at 12-months follow-up. Conversely, those who continued to binge eat did not lose weight. Another study (Agras, Telch, Arnow, Eldredge, & Marnell, 1997) found that abstinence from binge eating after a treatment approach that combined CBT and weight loss treatment was associated with sustained weight loss 1 year posttreatment, compared with weight gain in those who were not abstinent. At least for those in whom BED treatment achieves complete remission from binge eating, such treatment may have a positive impact on weight loss and weight maintenance.

These data suggest that one potential strategy for treating obese patients may be to use a combination approach that results in increasing weight loss during treatment and decreasing weight regain posttreatment. The optimal sequence, type of therapy, and patient characteristics remain to be determined through further research. The potential for exercise to reduce binge eating and to enhance weight maintenance also deserves further study (Pendleton, Goodrick, Poston, Reeves, & Foreyt, 2002).

Our challenge in the future is to understand better the ways in which BED and obesity coexist and to find treatment strategies that will relieve the distress and dysfunction due to the disordered eating, as well as enhance appropriate weight loss or, at a minimum, prevent further weight gain. Ultimately, early intervention in individuals at risk for BED could be one component in a strategy to prevent the development of overweight and obesity.

References

Agras, W.S., Telch, C.F., Arnow, B., Eldredge, K., & Marnell, M. (1997). One-year follow-up of cognitive-behavioral therapy for obese individuals with binge eating disorder. *Journal of Consulting and Clinical Psychology, 65,* 343–347.

Alger, S.A., Malone, M., Cerulli, J., Fein, S., & Howard, L. (1999). Beneficial effects of pharmacotherapy on weight loss, depressive symptoms, and eating patterns in obese binge eaters and non-binge eaters. *Obesity Research*, 7, 469–476.

de Zwaan, M. (2001). Binge eating disorder and obesity. *International Journal of Obesity and Related Metabolic Disorders*, 25 (Suppl.) 1, S51–S55.

Dingemans, A.E., Bruna, M.J., & van Furth, E.F. (2002). Binge eating disorder: A review. *International Journal of Obesity and Related Metabolic Disorders*, 26, 299–307.

Fairburn, C.G., Cooper, Z., Doll, H.A., Norman, P., & O'Connor, M. (2000). The natural course of bulimia nervosa and binge eating disorder in young women. *Archives of General Psychiatry*, 57, 659–665.

Fairburn, C.G., Welch, S.L., & Hay, P.J. (1993). The classification of recurrent overeating: The "binge eating disorder" proposal. *International Journal of Eating Disorders*, 13, 155–159.

Flegal, K.M., Carroll, M.D., Ogden, C.L., & Johnson, C.L. (2002). Prevalence and trends in obesity among US adults, 1999–2000. *Journal of the American Medical Association*, 288, 1723–1727.

Freedman, D.S., Khan, L.K., Serdula, M.K., Galuska, D.A., & Dietz, W.H. (2002). Trends and correlates of class 3 obesity in the United States from 1990 through 2000. *Journal of the American Medical Association*, 288, 1758–1761.

Gladis, M.M., Wadden, T.A., Vogt, R.A., Foster, G.D., Kuehnel, R.H., & Bartlett, S.J. (1998). Behavioral treatment of obese binge eaters: do they need different care? *Journal of Psychosomatic Research*, 44, 375–384.

Hsu, L.K., Mulliken, B., McDonagh, B., Krupa, D.S., Rand, W., Fairburn, C.G., Rolls, B., McCrory, M.A., Saltzman, E., Shikora, S., Dwyer, J., & Roberts, S. (2002). Binge eating disorder in extreme obesity. *International Journal of Obesity and Related Metabolic Disorders*, 26, 1398–1403.

Ogden, C.L., Flegal, K.M., Carroll, M.D., & Johnson, C.L. (2002). Prevalence and trends in overweight among US children and adolescents, 1999–2000. *Journal of the American Medical Association*, 288, 1728–1732.

Pendleton, V.R., Goodrick, G.K., Poston, W.S., Reeves, R.S., & Foreyt, J.P. (2002). Exercise augments the effects of cognitive-behavioral therapy in the treatment of binge eating. *International Journal of Eating Disorders*, 31, 172–184.

Shapira, N.A., Goldsmith, T.D., & McElroy, S.L. (2000). Treatment of binge-eating disorder with topiramate: a clinical case series. *Journal of Clinical Psychiatry*, 61, 368–372.

Sherwood, N.E., Jeffery, R.W., & Wing, R.R. (1999). Binge status as a predictor of weight loss treatment outcome. *International Journal of Obesity and Related Metabolic Disorders*, 23, 485–493.

Spitzer, R.L., Devlin, M., Walsh, B.T., Hasin, D., Wing, R., Marcus, M., Stunkard, A., Wadden, T., Yanovski, S., Agrass, S., Mitchell, J., & Nonas, C. (1992). Binge eating disorder: A multisite field trial of the diagnostic criteria. *International Journal of Eating Disorders*, 11, 191–203.

Spitzer, R.L., Yanovski, S., Wadden, T., Wing, R., Marcus, M.D., Stunkard, A., Devlin, M., Mitchell, J., Hasin, D., & Horne, R.L. (1993). Binge eating disorder: its further validation in a multisite study. *International Journal of Eating Disorders*, 13, 137–153.

Stukard, A. (2000). Two eating disorders: Binge eating disorder and the night eating syndrome. *Appetite*, 34, 333–334.

Stunkard, A.J. (1959). Eating patterns and obesity. *Psychological Bulletin*, 33, 284–294.

Stunkard, A.J., Berkowitz, R.I., Tanrikut, C., Reiss, E., & Young, L. (1996). d-Fenfluramine treatment of binge eating disorder. *American Journal of Psychiatry*, 153, 1455–1459.

Wadden, T.A., Brownell, K.D., & Foster, G.D. (2002). Obesity: responding to the global epidemic. *Journal of Consulting and Clinical Psychology*, 70, 510–525.

Wilfley, D.E., Welch, R.R., Stein, R.I., Spurrell, E.B., Cohen, L.R., Saelens, B.E., Dounchis, J.Z., Frank, M.A., Wiseman, C.V., & Matt, G.E. (2002). A randomized comparison of group cognitive-behavioral therapy and group interpersonal psychotherapy for the treatment of overweight individuals with binge-eating disorder. *Archives of General Psychiatry*, 59, 713–721.

Yanovski, S.Z. (1999). Diagnosis and prevalence of eating disorders in obesity. In B. Guy-Grand & G. Ailhaud (Eds.), *Progress in Obesity Research* (pp. 229–236). London: Libby.

Yanovski, S.Z., Gormally, J.F., Lesser, M.S., Gwirtsman, H.E., & Yanovski, J.A. (1994). Binge eating disorder affects outcome of comprehensive very-low-calorie diet treatment. *Obesity Research*, 2, 205–212.

"Twenty-five percent of those who diet develop partial or full syndrome eating disorders."

The Obesity Epidemic Is a Myth That Promotes Eating Disorders

Courtney E. Martin

Reports of an epidemic of obesity in America amount to scare tactics and hysteria, according to Courtney E. Martin in the following viewpoint. Martin charges that equating fat with sickness only drives people to unhealthy dieting cycles, dissatisfaction with one's body, and ultimately, full-blown eating disorders. Courtney E. Martin, a writer, teacher, and filmmaker in Brooklyn, New York, is the author of the book Perfect Girls, Starving Daughters.

As you read, consider the following questions:

1. Which industries serve to benefit from sensationalistic claims of an obesity epidemic, according to Martin?

2. As reported by the author, how has the percentage of high-school-aged girls who believe themselves to be overweight changed from 1995 to the present?

3. According to the 2006 *Ellegirl* poll cited by Martin, what percentage of respondents would rather be thin than healthy?

If you watch any mainstream news, you know that apparently America is in the midst of an obesity epidemic. Fear-producing news segments feature footage of overweight men and women, cut off at the heads like criminals, lumbering along the streets in Anytown, U.S.A. Ads with skinny women touting weight loss miracles as they look disdainfully at old pictures of their fatter, sadder selves run on a continuous loop on daytime television.

The scare tactics are working. Americans continue to pump billions, and blood, sweat, and tears into their "body projects," convinced that if they are fat, they are doomed.

Conflating fat with sickness is a dangerous delusion. The truth about fat, reinforced [in 2006] by a $419 million federal study involving 49,000 women, is that it does not automatically indicate unhealthiness. Many thin people, who don't exercise or eat balanced diets, are at a greater risk for disease than those with some extra padding who work out and eat relatively right. Your health can only be improved by movement and moderation. That's it. The study, published in the *Journal of the American Medical Association* [in February 2006], concludes that low-fat diets do not, despite all of the hype, reduce a woman's risk of cancer or heart disease.

Being fat is not equivalent to being unfit. In fact, being underweight actually kills over 30,000 Americans a year. Equating weight loss, instead of lifestyle changes, with improved health is "like saying 'whiter teeth produced by the elimination of smoking reduces the incidence of lung cancer,'" argues J. Eric Oliver, author of *Fat Politics: The Real Story Behind America's Obesity Epidemic*. Even a group of CDC [Centers for Disease Control and Prevention] researchers admit that "evidence that weight loss improves survival is limited."

So why do highly educated, media-savvy Americans continue to buy into the idea that the thinner one is, the healthier and happier one is? The mammoth diet industry, not to mention the exercise, beauty, fashion, and cosmetic surgery industries, certainly has something to do with it. In America, alone, we spend $40 billion annually on diet products, even though diets prove to be ineffective 95 percent of the time. Not only is our stupidity disturbing—those stakes wouldn't even lure the drunkest of Vegas gamblers—but the implications are foreboding.

Fear of Fat Pushes People into Eating Disorders

There is a slippery slope from dieting to disease, as the 7 million girls and women suffering from eating disorders in this country will attest. Thirty-five percent of those who diet go on to yo-yo diet, dragging their bodies through a cycle of weight gains and losses far more unhealthy than just being overweight; 25 percent of those who diet develop partial or full syndrome eating disorders. Mindfulness advocate Susan Albers writes: "The dieting mindset is akin to taking a knife and cutting the connection that is your body's only line of communication with your head." There is little hope for long-term health improvement with this vital line severed.

Cut off from our ability to listen to our authentic hungers, we ride a roller coaster of marketed cravings and emotional upheaval—overeating, then guiltily undereating, then overeating again. But unlike brief and thrilling amusement park adventures, we can't seem to get off the ride. The explosion of coverage on "the obesity epidemic," though well-intentioned, has not served as the emergency break nutritionists and doctors so hoped it would. Instead, the sensational news spots on the dangers of obesity have often fed misperceptions about the direct link between fat and unhealthiness, or worse, fat and unworthiness.

Hysteria over Fat Goes Hand-in-Hand with the Anorexic Mindset

It is no exaggeration to say that in many respects contemporary America is a fundamentally eating-disordered culture. A much-noted sign of this can be seen in the binge-sized portions that are now standard fare in our restaurants and fast-food emporia. A less-noted piece of evidence is provided by the almost overtly anorexic quality of much of the current hysteria about fat.

One explanation for the remarkable distortions of the medical evidence in which those who prosecute the case against fat indulge is that many of these people see that evidence through anorexic eyes. Let me be clear: I am not claiming that all such persons are technically anorexic (although some undoubtedly are). What I am saying is that the anorexic mindset is far more common than our narrow definition of what constitutes instances of the syndrome itself, and that this mindset has played an important part in producing America's growing intolerance of even the mildest forms of body diversity.

Consider that anyone who attends a conference on the "obesity epidemic" in America today is likely to find that a good number of the participants are extremely thin, high-achieving, upper-class white women, many of whom appear to have both strong perfectionist tendencies and a pathological fear and loathing of fat. Any accurate account of the war on fat must grapple with the fact that many obesity researchers, eating disorder specialists, nutritionists and so on belong to the precise social groups that are at the highest risk for anorexia nervosa—and that indeed a significant number of these individuals display at least some of the classic symptoms of the syndrome.

Paul Campos, "The Obesity Myth,"
Spiked Online, *October 7, 2005.*

Hyperbolic reportage on the expanding waistlines of America's children, in particular, has created a damaging hysteria. Fat camps are flooded with applicants who are solidly within their recommended body weight. In 1995, 34 percent of high school-aged girls in the U.S. thought they were overweight. Today, 90 percent do. And those who really are fat, and yes, there are many, are subjected to increasing scrutiny and scolding. The fat kid in school, once the butt of mean jokes, is now the target of a societal assault. A recent survey of parents found that 1 in 10 would abort a child if they found out that he or she had a genetic tendency to be fat.

We are being brainwashed by sensationalistic news segments and the 250 ads we see a day that tell us, not only that fat is unhealthy, but a sign of weak character. In a recent poll by *Ellegirl* magazine of 10,000 readers, 30 percent said they would rather be thin than healthy. Over half the young women between the ages of 18 and 25 would prefer to be run over by a truck than be fat, and two-thirds surveyed would rather be mean or stupid. The single group of teenagers most likely to consider or attempt suicide is girls who worry that they are overweight.

The messages are coming in loud and clear, and they are riddled with disempowering dichotomies—all or nothing, feast or famine, disgustingly fat or virtuously thin, deeply flawed or triumphantly perfect. There is no talk of what Buddhists describe as "the middle path," no discussion of the pleasure of walking, eating homemade food, slowing down. There is no permission to say "no" sometimes and "yes" sometimes, and have those no's and yeses be simple answers, insignificant scores on a Scrabble board, representative of nothing more than a mood. Instead our yeses and no's signify our desirability, our life expectancy, our self-worth.

Reject Extreme Attitudes Toward Food and Weight

It is not fat itself that is unhealthy, but our hypocritical attitudes and compulsive behaviors that are. We drive two blocks

63

to the grocery store and then spend 20 minutes circling the parking lot so we can get a close spot. Once inside we load up our carts with low-fat, microwave meals and diet shakes filled with artificial everything. In the checkout line, we read about the latest fitness trend in *Men's Health* or *Self*, then get back into our cars, drive the two blocks home, and sit in front of the tevision all night eating Pizza Hut while drinking a liter of Diet Coke. We go to bed late, wake up early, head to work—in our cars, of course—where we will spend the next eight hours stationary and bored. Rinse. Repeat.

We don't need expensive, genetically engineered foods or state-of-the-art exercise equipment. We don't need fancy doctors or pharmaceutical drugs. We don't need the latest diet craze book or even the latest medical study—they all seem to contradict each other anyway. We don't even need Herculean willpower.

We just need to leave our cars in the garage, stroll down to the park, and play some softball with our neighbors on a Saturday. We just need to enjoy every last bite of our home-baked birthday cakes, then have some oatmeal for breakfast the next morning. We need to resist the pressure to overwork and underenjoy. If we want to live long, healthy, happy lives, then we need to stop believing the hype. We need to rediscover our own wise instincts that know far more about well-being than a whole country of experts.

Periodical Bibliography

The following articles have been selected to supplement the diverse views presented in this chapter.

Kelly C. Allison and
Jennifer D. Lundgren
"Eating Disorders in Obese Individuals," *Obesity Management*, vol. 2, no. 3, June 2006, pp. 110–13.

Margena A. Christian
"What Black Women Need to Know About Eating Disorders," *Jet*, September 25, 2006, pp. 28–30.

Andrea Faiad
"Dying to Be Thin: Eating Disorders Are Ugly. Here's Why," *Current Health*, November 2006, pp. 20–24.

HealthyPlace.com
"Eating Disorders in Males," 2005. www.healthyplace.com/Communities/ Eating_Disorders/men_2.asp.

James Hudson et al.
"The Prevalence and Correlates of Eating Disorders in the National Comorbidity Survey," *Biological Psychiatry*, vol. 61, no. 3, February 1, 2007, pp. 348–58.

Michelle Lodge
"Thin Gray Line," *Time*, October 30, 2006, Bonus Section, p. 9.

Diana Mahoney
"The Many Ironies of Eating Disorders," *Clinical Psychiatry News*, April 2006, p. 52.

David Luc Nguyen
"Wasting Away: What's Driving Young Gay Men to Starve, Binge, and Purge?" *Advocate*, September 26, 2006, p. 24.

Lynn Santa Lucia
"Driven to Be Thin: Millions of Teens Suffer from Eating Disorders and Many of Them Are Boys," *Scholastic Choices*, September 2006, pp. 20–27.

Amanda Smith
"The Mirror Has Two Faces: Dancers Have a Special Vulnerability to Eating Disorders," *Dance*, July 2006, pp. 34–36.

OPPOSING VIEWPOINTS® SERIES

CHAPTER 2

What Causes Eating Disorders?

Chapter Preface

Eating disorders (EDs) have confounded therapists since the nineteenth century, and the debate over the relative significance of several possible causes remains unresolved. News from the international fashion industry in 2006 and 2007 refocused attention on one presumed cause, cultural attitudes that equate extreme thinness and beauty, and the role of such attitudes in triggering EDs.

The subject first made headlines in August 2006, when Uruguayan model Luisel Ramos, age twenty-two, collapsed and died shortly after stepping off a runway at a Montevideo fashion show. At five feet, nine inches, she weighed ninety-eight pounds, and her heart failure was widely attributed to an eating disorder. In September, the organizers of the annual Cibeles Fashion Show in Madrid enacted the first-ever ban on underweight models, reacting to charges that high-profile fashion designers' increasing use of ultrathin models on the catwalk promoted eating disorders in young women trying to copy the stick-thin look. Modeling agencies and designers objected, arguing that superskinny fashion models were naturally "gazelle-like," not unhealthy, and charging that the ban violated models' and designers' right to pursue their profession.

Then in November 2006, another model, twenty-one-year-old Brazilian Ana Carolina Reston, died of complications associated with anorexia; at five feet, eight inches, she reportedly weighed eighty-eight pounds at the time of her death. Fashion industry claims that models are naturally thin rang hollow when Reston's mother stated publicly that her daughter had repeatedly been told she was too "obese" for runway work and had had to starve herself to be hired.

In November and December, newspapers carried stories of the deaths of three more young Brazilian women suffering from anorexia, and criticism of the fashion industry as irresponsible promoters of eating disorders intensified. The sponsors of Milan's Fashion Week followed Madrid's lead and required models to submit to yearly physicals and prove their weight fell within normal limits or be banned from participation. In January 2007 the Academy for Eating Disorders urged the international fashion industry to adopt a comprehensive set of guidelines including:

- Adoption of an age threshold requiring that models be at least 16 years old so as to reduce the pressure that adolescent girls feel to conform to the ultra-thin standard of female beauty.

- For women and men over the age of 18, adoption of a minimum body mass index threshold of 18.5 kg/m^2 (e.g., a female model who is 5'9" [1.75 m] must weigh more than 126 pounds [57.3 kg]). . . .

- A ban on the use of photographic manipulation techniques that artificially slim images of fashion models. . . .

The organizers of London's and New York's Fashion Weeks, however, refused to explicitly ban abnormally thin models from their February 2007 events, instead issuing voluntary guidelines that urged designers and show producers to hire healthy models. As images of startlingly thin models were circulated on the Internet, in newspapers, and on television in 2007, fashion industry representatives continued to portray designers as scapegoats and eating disorder professionals continued to express concern that these images set a terrible example for millions of girls who dream of modeling careers or view fashion models as the most beautiful women in the world. And in mid-February 2007, eighteen-year-old Uruguayan model Eliana Ramos, the sister of Luisel Ramos, died in Montevideo of malnutrition attributed to anorexia.

The viewpoints in the following chapter examine the genetic, neurological, psychological, and social factors that influence the development of eating disorders and debate their relative significance.

| "[International research studies] have
been surprisingly consistent in showing
a substantial genetic contribution to
anorexia nervosa and bulimia nervosa."

Genetics Play a Significant Role in Eating Disorders

Craig Johnson and Cynthia Bulik

In late 2002 the National Institute of Mental Health funded a landmark five-year study of the genetics of anorexia, conducted by eleven research groups across North America and Europe. In the following viewpoint, principal investigators Craig Johnson and Cynthia Bulik give twin-study evidence that hereditary factors explain why eating disorders run in families. The authors maintain that when the relevant genes are identified—theoretically single-gene mutations but more likely multiple-gene interactions—prevention and treatment efforts can be targeted to at-risk individuals. Craig Johnson is the founder and director of the eating disorders program at Laureate Psychiatric Clinic and Hospital in Tulsa, Oklahoma, associate professor of psychiatry at the University of Oklahoma College of Medicine, and past presi-

Craig Johnson and Cynthia Bulik, "Brave New World: The Role of Genetics in the Prevention and Treatment of Eating Disorders," a Collaborative Study of the Genetics of Anorexia Nervosa and Bulimia Nervosa, University of Pittsburgh Medical Center, November 6, 2002. www.wpic.pitt.edu/research/pfanbn/genetics.html. Reproduced by permission.

dent of the National Eating Disorders Association. Cynthia Bulik is William R. Jordan Distinguished Professor of Eating Disorders in the Department of Psychiatry and director of the Eating Disorders Program at the University of North Carolina at Chapel Hill.

As you read, consider the following questions:

1. What is the elevated risk of developing anorexia or bulimia in a person whose mother or sister has suffered from anorexia, according to the authors?
2. How can twin studies indicate whether an eating disorder is genetically or environmentally influenced, according to Johnson and Bulik?
3. Which genetically linked personality traits do Johnson and Bulik say might predispose an individual to developing an eating disorder?

The completion of the Human Genome Project has drawn widespread attention to the rapidly accelerating field of genetic research. Interestingly, significant genetic work has been occurring in the eating disorders field that has not been sufficiently shared with the public. One of the largest contributions in this area of research comes from a collaborative group of investigators under the leadership of Principal Investigator Walter Kaye, M.D. The Collaborative Group includes both sites in the US and several international research sites that have been conducting state-of-the-art genetic research related to eating disorders [since 1998].

Relative Risk

The exploration of possible genetic factors contributing to eating disorders is well founded. It has been observed for decades that eating disorders often run in families. Even when relatives of a woman with an eating disorder have not been clinically diagnosed as suffering from an eating disorder, many clinicians often hear tales from patients about relatives displaying traits associated with eating disorders. Clients may recall mothers, aunts, or fathers who were "obsessed with weight," "ate like a bird," or "hated their appearance."

Formal family studies have shown that relatives of individuals with eating disorders are at substantially greater risk for developing eating disorders themselves. This is commonly referred to as significantly elevated relative risk. In fact, preliminary studies indicate that family members of someone with anorexia nervosa are twelve times more likely to develop an eating disorder than relatives of someone without anorexia nervosa. Thus, eating disorders rank among the most familial of psychiatric disorders.

In spite of a general awareness that family influences impact eating disorders sufferers, clinical observation and family studies are unable to determine why eating disorders run in families. An understanding that family members model disordered eating behaviors and attitudes would suggest environmental transmission. Alternatively, or in addition, the familial pattern could also be due to genetic factors. Twin studies have shed some light on this nature vs. nurture debate.

Twin Studies

The study of twins offers the unique opportunity to examine the extent to which the transmission of a disorder in families is due to environmental or genetic factors. Identical twins share all of their genes and fraternal twins share, on average, half of their genes. If a disorder occurs in both members of identical twin pairs more often than it occurs in both members of fraternal twin pairs, then that is the first hint that the disorder may be influenced by genes.

In the study of genetic influence, the term *shared environment* refers to those aspects of environment that are shared by both members of a twin pair such as socioeconomic status,

"Candidate Genes"
Possibly Linked to Eating Disorders

In a genetic association study, candidate genes that are suggested to be involved in the pathophysiology of the disease can be investigated for their role in the onset of the trait. In such studies, the allele or genotype frequencies at markers, single nucleotide polymorphisms (SNP), are determined in affected individuals and compared to those of controls (either population- or family-based). Association studies are known as an effective approach to detect the effect of variants within candidate genes with relatively small effects. . . .

[From 1995 to 2005] the number of studies focusing on the role of genetics in the etiology of eating disorders . . . increased enormously. This increase has been met by some successes in molecular genetic studies, although the majority of results remain inconclusive. Genome-wide screens have demonstrated linkage peaks for AN and BN on chromosomes 1p33–36, 4q13, 10p13 and 14q22–23. Furthermore, one collaborative study has incorporated behavioral covariates into their linkage analyses and identified three additional suggestive linkage peaks (chromosome 1q31, 2p11 and 13q13). To confirm the linkage findings, further replication studies are needed.

Margarita C.T. Slof-Op't Landt et al., "Eating Disorders:
From Twin Studies to Candidate Genes and Beyond,"
Twin Research and Human Genetics,
vol. 8, no. 5, October 2005, pp. 467–82.

religion, and general parenting style. These influences act to make twins more similar. The term *unique environment*, in contrast, refers to those environmental influences that are experienced by only one member of a twin pair (e.g., trauma, participating in sports that emphasize thinness). Those experiences serve to make twins more different. Several population-based twin studies have been conducted in Virginia, Australia, Denmark, Sweden, Norway, Finland, and Minnesota and have addressed the genetic and environmental factors which contribute to the development of anorexia and bulimia nervosa. These studies have also examined genetic and environmental influences on related traits such as drive for thinness and body dissatisfaction. The results have been surprisingly consistent in showing a substantial genetic contribution to anorexia nervosa and bulimia nervosa as well as to the traits that are associated with these disorders. When the environmental influences are considered together, the unique environmental effects have greater impact than the shared environmental effects on liability to developing eating disorders.

Single Genes Versus Multiple Genes?

Although twin studies offer consistent support for the notion that genes contribute to the development of eating disorders, they cannot help us unravel which genes are implicated and how they actually influence risk. Like other behavioral disorders, anorexia and bulimia nervosa are complex disorders. This means that they are likely to be caused by multiple genes and multiple environmental factors of small to moderate effect, unlike monogenic diseases (caused by one gene) such as Huntington's disease.

Obesity is a complex trait that has been studied extensively from a genetic perspective. There have been several single-gene mutations identified that lead to rare forms of obesity. However, taken together, these single-gene mutations only account for a small percentage of obesity cases. Future research dedicated to examining the risk for obesity will no doubt lead to the understanding of multiple genes and environmental variables that may influence obesity such as sedentary lifestyle, high fat diets, and overeating.

It is theoretically possible that single-gene mutations might exist which result in anorexia, bulimia, or other disordered eating (e.g., a mutation that affects the functioning of the hypothalamus, which plays a major role in hunger and satiety). However, it is more likely that, as with obesity, there will be multiple genes interacting with environmental variables. To date, we have identified areas on chromosome 1 (anorexia nervosa) and chromosome 10 (bulimia nervosa) that may harbor susceptibility loci for these disorders.

For anorexia nervosa, genes could influence traits such as the ability to maintain an extremely low body weight or having a constitutionally high activity level. They could also influence personality or psychopathological traits such as perfectionism, anxiety proneness, obsessionality, fear of new situations, and low self-esteem. However, even if an individual was at high genetic risk (i.e., possessed several of these relevant genes), she might never develop anorexia nervosa if she did not live in a culture such as ours which emphasizes dieting and thinness. So called gene environment interaction may be the operative mechanism whereby an individual's genetic risk becomes expressed.

Targeting At-Risk Individuals

Although the above considerations are presented as speculation, it is clear that a better understanding of the genetic contribution to eating disorders might inform and improve both prevention and treatment efforts. If genes that play a causal role in eating disorders can be identified, we will then be able to identify at-risk individuals with greater precision. Once relevant genes are identified, researchers and health professionals could theoretically be able to quantify risk more accurately. Currently, the best method for identifying high-risk individuals is the consideration of family history as well as environmental factors such as peer influence, participation in high-risk sports or activities, dieting behaviors, etc. Given that widespread prevention efforts have not eliminated eating disorders altogether, more targeted prevention directed towards those who are genetically vulnerable could be more effective and definitely more efficient. Furthermore, with the identification of genes, could also come the unveiling of biological pathways that lead to disordered eating behaviors. This could lead to the identification of "druggable targets" that could lead to medications that are effective in the treatment of eating disorders.

For now, as we have not yet reached the point of being able to identify specific genes that influence risk, we must focus our preventive efforts on the environment. Reducing exposure to environmental risk factors and enhancing exposure to buffering environmental factors may be helpful in reducing the likelihood of expression of an underlying genetic predisposition. When eating disorders do develop, early detection and treatment improve the odds of full recovery.

> "The phenomenon of anorexia nervosa ... may just be predictable, instinctive responses to undiagnosed digestive tract disorders."

Eating Disorders May Be Symptoms of Chronic Physical Illness

Randy Schellenberg

Randy Schellenberg is a businessman in British Columbia. In June 2001 his eighth-grade daughter was diagnosed with anorexia nervosa and underwent several months of fruitless psychotherapy and two eating-disorder hospitalizations before her gall bladder condition was correctly diagnosed and surgery cured her illness. In the following viewpoint, Schellenberg criticizes the standard criteria for the diagnosis of anorexia and charges that medical professionals too often fail to rule out physical illness before making eating disorder diagnoses.

As you read, consider the following questions:

1. Why does Schellenberg say one *DSM-IV* criteria for anorexia nervosa, intense fear of gaining weight, is too subjective?

Randy Schellenberg, "Anorexic and Bulimic Patients Urged to Insist on Diagnostic Testing to Rule Out Medical Illness," Anorexia Truth.com, summer 2006. Reproduced by permission.

2. How could disturbances in one's perception of one's own body weight or shape actually be the result of physical illness and not anorexia nervosa, according to the author?

3. What medical conditions does the author cite as alternatives to anorexia as causes of amenorrhea?

The latest research suggests that the phenomenon of anorexia nervosa [AN] may not be strictly a psychiatric disorder, but rather for many may just be predictable, instinctive responses to undiagnosed digestive tract disorders. There may be many patients in eating disorder programs who are actually suffering from chronic medical disorders rather than mental illness. Current treatment protocols involving refeeding and behavioral therapy have often had poor outcomes, with a high rate of morbidity, mortality, and high rates of suicide.

Unfortunately, the belief that anorexia nervosa and its close cousin Bulimia are strictly psychiatric disorders is so entrenched among psychotherapists, nutritionists, and physicians, that in many cases proper diagnostic studies are not being performed to rule out underlying medical disorders.

Those who have a chronic digestive or metabolic disorder may not realize it, and when they start a strenuous exercise program, begin a diet, or experience the increased caloric demands of puberty, they may not develop an appropriate appetite for their energy requirements. Conversely, athletes, dancers, figure skaters or models who maintain strict diet and exercise regimens may be vulnerable to dangerous weight loss due to medical illness if the condition is not properly diagnosed and treated. Severe malnutrition may ensue due to inadequate caloric intake or reduced absorption while trying to maintain their training regimen. . . .

To understand why it is so easy for a person with a digestive disorder to be misdiagnosed as having AN, it is necessary to take a critical look at the diagnostic criteria of DSM-IV

Many Medical Illnesses Can Be Misdiagnosed as Anorexia

A wide variety of medical problems can masquerade as eating disorders. Hyperthyroidism, malignancy, inflammatory bowel disease, immunodeficiency, malabsorption, chronic infections, Addison's disease, and diabetes should be considered before making a diagnosis of an eating disorder. Most patients with a medical condition that leads to eating problems express concern over their weight loss. However, patients with an eating disorder have a distorted body image and express a desire to be underweight.

Sarah D. Pritts and Jeffrey Susman,
"Diagnosis of Eating Disorders in Primary Care,"
American Family Physician, *vol. 67, 2003, pp. 297–304, 311–12.*

[the *Diagnostic and Statistical Manual of Mental Disorders*, which sets four criteria for the diagnosis of anorexia nervosa]. If the anorexic patient fulfills all of these criteria, then AN is diagnosed. After that, generally little or no effort will be made to search for physical causes of appetite loss. Let's examine each part of the criteria:

Refusal to Maintain Body Weight

It is easy to interpret the refusal to eat as something the patient is purposely doing to achieve some sort of weight goal. Yet most anorexic patients just don't feel like eating. Of course, if you assume that the patient is in perfect health (besides being malnourished), then not eating appears to be a deliberate choice. It is not that simple. Physical illness can severely impact appetite, and also absorption. So to conclusively determine that the patient is consciously refusing to maintain their body weight within 15% of normal (this is also a subjective matter) one has to eliminate every possibility of appetite loss due to disease. Some diseases that cause appetite loss, nausea, or malabsorption are very easy to diagnose, and usually the patient will know something's wrong. Others, especially chronic diseases, are not and may require extensive diagnostic testing to identify.

Intense Fear of Gaining Weight or Becoming Fat

The adjective "intense" is highly subjective. The majority of women are very conscious of their figures. This is not necessarily a bad thing. Almost everyone, male or female, who interacts socially with other people is somewhat self-conscious with regards to their appearance (most of us look in the mirror and comb our hair before we go to school or work).

This criteria is the one that is prone to making women much more likely to be misdiagnosed with AN than a man. Let's assume the prevalence of chronic digestive disorders is the same among men and women (this would be an incorrect assumption, as the prevalence of many diseases varies with gender). Because women in general are far more concerned about being overweight than men (men typically would like to be more muscular or stronger), they will be far more likely to fulfill this criteria.

Young women are far more likely to wear tight-fitting clothes (example: "painted-on" jeans) and so will notice even slight fluctuations in weight or fluid retention. A young woman can become quite frustrated that she won't fit in her tight jeans for several days each month, and if this is due to fluid retention or bloating she may "feel" fat as well.

Just how "intense" does this fear of gaining weight have to be? If the patient doesn't at first acknowledge this fear, will the therapist try to persuade her to admit to this fear? Certainly, if the therapist believes that the diagnosis should be AN, the temptation to extract a confession of weight preoccupation will be very strong. Once the patient does admit to being concerned about her weight, will this fulfill the criteria?

Disturbance in the Way in Which One's Body Weight or Shape Is Experienced

When we look at someone other than ourselves, we tend not to be as critical of their appearance as we are of our own. When we look in the mirror, we may focus on details of our appearance that we would not focus on with others. If we have a painful pimple on our forehead, we may focus our attention on it and even become distressed about it. Others may not even notice it. This is because we are far more conscious of self than of others.

We also can experience pain or discomfort that may make us overly conscious of certain parts of our anatomy. Such may be the case if a person has a digestive disorder that causes abdominal bloating and distension.

The discomfort of bloating can command the sufferer's attention, and if the cause of this condition is not recognized, it may be interpreted as fat. Certainly, abdominal distension can make you feel and look fat, and the inability to fit into clothes may be convincing evidence for some. Most eating disorder programs only monitor weight and height. They generally do not monitor waist size, nor abdominal distension. This distension may be transient, varying with diet and stage of digestion. They also generally do not monitor edema (water retention) and its effects on the patient's interpretation of their body shape.

The therapist may ask the anorexic patient to choose from several frontal silhouettes of thin, medium build, and obese bodies, that which most closely resembles their own. If the patient chooses the obese silhouette, this may be interpreted as confirmation of distorted body image perception. Of course an emaciated, malnourished anorexic patient is not fat. But it is perfectly understandable that she may feel fat. And as she loses weight and becomes more emaciated, her stomach by comparison looks even bigger. This optical illusion can convince the anorexic patient that more stomach crunches are needed or that they have to lose more weight.

Denial of the Seriousness of the Current Low Body Weight

The human body has an amazing ability to adapt to a wide range of conditions. This probably explains why the human species has survived for so long. Conditioning plays a key role in this adaptive response. If we lift heavy loads on a regular basis, our muscles grow bigger and stronger to handle the increased demand. If we take up jogging, our heart becomes stronger and more efficient to more effectively handle the demands placed on it. Some people who start jogging may only be able to make it half way around the block at first, but through conditioning may be able to run a marathon after a year of training.

The adaptive response to starvation is a truly amazing phenomenon, one that has secured the survival of the species through many famines over the course of history. If malnutrition sets in gradually, over the course of a few months or a few years, the body gradually adapts to the new conditions. The malnourished person may still have energy, and not feel lethargic or sickly. You'll find that most anorexic individuals indeed have very high energy levels, despite being seriously malnourished. In fact, there may be a natural tendency to be hyperactive, as the brain, preoccupied with sourcing nutrition, makes an effort to provide every survival advantage. In terms of evolutionary biology, this hyperactive state would have increased the prospects of starving populations catching elusive game or travelling to an area with a better food supply. If the anorexic patient has a digestive disorder, they may find it impossible to eat, and yet be totally adapted to their advanced state of malnutrition as well as their digestive disorder. Due to this adaptive response, the patient may not realize the seriousness of their condition.

Amenorrhea in Postmenarcheal Females

It is pertinent to note that anorexia nervosa is the only psychiatric disorder with a physical symptom as one of the diagnostic criteria. This is another criteria that causes much confusion both among therapists and physicians. Many physicians interpret the cessation of menses as one more symptom of AN. However, it is not that simple.

Amenorrhea may have many causes, including hypothyroidism, adrenal tumor, congenital abnormalities, polycycstic ovary or ovarian tumor. These possible causes must be ruled out through diagnostic testing before a diagnosis can be made. Malnutrition or excessive exercise can also cause amenorrhea. If AN is suspected, the amenorrhea is normally assumed to be due to malnutrition. Of course, the malnutrition is usually assumed to be due to a willful refusal to eat, in other words, anorexia nervosa. You can see how these assumptions become dangerous, because a female with a digestive disorder may also refuse to eat and become malnourished, and experience amenorrhea.

You can see how the diagnostic criteria from DSM-IV are totally inadequate to rule out physical causes of anorexia. Symptoms and behaviors assumed to be associated with AN can all be caused by chronic digestive tract disorders. All criteria are too subjective and are very prone to misinterpretation. It is no wonder there has been such an explosion in the prevalence of anorexia nervosa. The psychiatric community must address these deficiencies with the utmost urgency to prevent further misdiagnoses.

> *"Anorexia [is] a disorder based in biology, specifically in the appetite regulation mechanism in the brain."*

Neurochemical Imbalances Cause Anorexia

Ellen Ruppel Shell

In the following viewpoint, science journalist Ellen Ruppel Shell presents psychologist Shan Guisinger's theory that anorexia originated in ancient humans as an advantageous adaptation that aided survival during migrations and food scarcity. Being able to "starve well," some experts agree, is hardwired into the brain, and environmental factors may trigger the same appetite suppression in modern-day anorexics. Ellen Ruppel Shell, a regular contributor to Atlantic Monthly *and the* New York Times Magazine, *is codirector of the Science Journalism Program at Boston University.*

As you read, consider the following questions:

1. What behaviors in whales and laboratory rats does the author compare to human anorexic behavior to support the claim that anorexia is based in biology?

Ellen Ruppel Shell, "The Ancestry of Anorexia: Blame Biology, Not Parenting, New Theory Suggests," *Boston Globe*, December 30, 2003. www.boston.com/yourlife/health/mental/articles/2003/12/30/the_ancestry_of_anorexia/. Copyright © 2003 Globe Newspaper Company. Reproduced by permission of the author.

2. According to Shell, why is psychological treatment for anorexia doomed to fail without addressing physiological aspects of the disorder?

3. What brain chemicals does Shell identify in connection with anorexia, and what are the effects of high or low levels of these chemicals?

Anorexia, the most lethal of psychiatric disorders, afflicts as many as 1 percent of young women and about a tenth as many men, and casts a Svengalian spell, leading its victims to willingly starve themselves in the midst of plenty. Now, psychologist Shan Guisinger has developed a radical new view of anorexia that she says explains both the bizarre features of the illness—self starvation and hyperactivity—and its resistance to treatment by traditional psychotherapy.

Anorexia, she contends, is not primarily a psychological condition brought on by a troubled childhood—as is often thought—but a disorder based in biology, specifically in the appetite regulation mechanism in the brain. Her theory postulates that anorexics have a biological adaptation to weight loss that causes their bodies to shut off hunger signals, and to ratchet up physical activity, even as their flesh melts away.

"Anorexics are often told to stop dieting, to listen to their body and to give it what it wants," Guisinger said. "But the reality is that they are listening to their bodies, and their bodies are telling them not to eat. The truth is, they have to stop listening."

Guisinger, who has treated eating disorders in private practice in Missoula, Mont., for nearly two decades, trained in evolutionary biology in the late 1970's before getting a doctorate in clinical psychology at the University of California at Berkeley. This background, coupled with her upbringing on a farm in Washington state, convinced her that Freudian and other purely psychological explanations for anorexia were inadequate.

"We sometimes forget that humans are animals first," she said, describing her theory, which she published [in 2003] in the prestigious *Journal of Psychological Review*. "And a number of animals are able to turn off hunger when they have something better to do." Gray whales, for example, won't eat while they're migrating, even if food is plentiful. Laboratory rats starved down to 70 percent of their body weight stop eating and become hyperactive, spinning up to 12 miles a day on their tiny exercise wheels.

Tracing Anorexia Back 11,000 Years

Guisinger's "Adapted to Flee Hypothesis" traces the roots of human anorexia back more than 11,000 years to the late Pleistocene era, when nomadic foragers migrated around the globe. At that time, the biological capacity to suppress hunger and move quickly and tirelessly in search of food may have offered an adaptive advantage, just as it appears to offer an advantage to migrating animals.

"Today, genetically susceptible people who lose a good deal of weight may trigger this archaic adaptation," she said. "And that's what underlies their illness."

Critics scoff that a potentially fatal disorder that suppresses fertility in women is hardly "adaptive." But Guisinger does not argue that anorexia per se helps an individual survive and reproduce in the modern world. Rather she says that anorexics suffer from a toxic distortion of the innate mechanisms that kept our ancient ancestors alive.

Daniel le Grange, director of an eating disorders program at the University of Chicago says Guisinger's idea has "a ring of truth about it, because those who survived [in ancient times] must have had a gene to allow them to starve well." Indeed, the very intractability of anorexia suggests that it had some adaptive function in human evolution: Being wired into the brain through eons of history, it is far less likely than learned behaviors to respond favorably to traditional psychotherapy.

Anorexia Is Linked to Serotonin Abnormalities in the Brain

[Editor's Note: Serotonin, known to researchers as 5-HT, is an important neurotransmitter, a brain chemical that regulates appetite, mood, vomiting, and sleep. Low levels of 5-HT have been linked to several psychiatric disorders.]

Appetite behavior is a complex system involving gastrointestinal function, hormonal, and peripheral and central nervous system pathways. In the brain, a cascade of monoamines and neuropeptide regulates aspects of feeding such as macronutrient selection, rate of eating, satiety, etc. Stereotypic feeding patterns in AN may be a consequence of specific neurochemical alterations. For example, a case can be made that 5-HT overactivity may contribute to exaggerated satiety in AN. Theoretically, food restriction could be caused by increased intra-synaptic 5-HT or activation of 5-HT receptors. . . .

Furthermore, pathologic eating behavior could be related to altered modulation of food-related reward mechanisms. Tastes, smells, foods, and flavors all consistently activate overlapping regions of the orbital frontal cortex, anterior cingulate cortex, antermedial temporal (including amygdala), and insula, which are regions implicated in AN and bulimia nervosa [BN]. These brain regions may modulate the reward value of a sensory stimulus such as the taste of food. Normally, food tastes pleasant when one is hungry. However, after one has eaten a food to satiety, there is a reduction in the pleasantness of its taste. Thus neurons in the orbital frontal cortex decrease their response to a food eaten to satiety but remain responsive to other foods, contributing to a mechanism for sensory-specific satiety. We hypothesize that women with AN and BN have a disturbance of these hedonic pathways. That is, for AN, there is little hedonic response to food, or rapid development of satiety. In contrast, BN may have exaggerated hedonic response to food, or little development of satiety, so that overeating follows.

Walter H. Kaye et al., "Neurobiology of Anorexia Nervosa: Clinical Implications of Alterations of the Function of Serotonin and Other Neuronal Systems," International Journal of Eating Disorders, *vol. 37, 2005, pp. S15–S19.*

Modern Research into Anorexics' Brain Chemistry

Walter Kaye, a psychiatrist and professor of psychiatry at the University of Pittsburgh says the physiological component of the illness is extremely powerful.

"Anorexia is a very homogeneous disorder," he said. "People who have it have about the same symptoms. They also tend to say the same things, act the same way. When you see that kind of pattern, it says biological."

Numerous scientific studies show that weight loss from any cause—be it dieting, depression, or even surgery or physical illness—can initiate the anorexic cycle in the genetically inclined. Nearly half its victims struggle with the disease throughout their lives.

Cynthia Bulik, a professor of psychiatry at the University of North Carolina at Chapel Hill who has studied anorexia since the mid-1980s, said that while important, psychological treatments for the disorder fail if they don't first address the physiological aspects. She points out that anorexics, like all starving people, tend to be unreliable witnesses of their own experience.

"You can't do deep psychotherapy with someone whose brain is not working," she said.

Anorexics have chronically high levels of cholecystokinin, serotonin, and dopamine, chemicals that signal satiety in the brain. They also have low levels of appetite promoters, such as galanin and norepinephrine. Hence their brains are chronically lying about the body's need for food, or at best passing on a distorted view.

Searching for the Genetic Basis of Neurochemical Imbalance

The National Institutes of Health is sponsoring a study to uncover the genetic variance underlying this neurochemical deception. The goal is both to predict who among us has the potential to become anorexic, and to sort out subsets of anorexics who may respond to various treatments.

Bernard Devlin, a statistical geneticist and professor of psychiatry at the University of Pittsburgh is, along with Kaye, one of the principal investigators in the NIH study. Part of his effort involves looking for the genes that make anorexics vulnerable to environmental triggers. "We have found some genomic regions that we believe are associated with behaviors that predict anorexia, and we're hoping to eventually narrow it down to specific genes, or combinations of genes," Devlin said.

"Understanding the symptoms of anorexia as an archaic biological adaptation can free psychotherapists, physicians, and parents from unjustified blaming," [Guisinger] said. "And that in itself is a big step toward curbing this devastating disease."

> "There are many theories, many interwoven factors, and no one simple answer that covers persons with an eating disorder."

Eating Disorders Have Multiple Complex Causes

Anorexia Nervosa and Related Eating Disorders, Inc.

The causes of eating disorders must be viewed as a mix of biological, psychological, social, and cultural factors, the Anorexia Nervosa and Related Eating Disorders foundation (ANRED) argues in the following viewpoint. The more risk factors a person has, ANRED warns, the higher the probability of developing an eating disorder. ANRED is a nonprofit organization founded in 1979 to combat eating disorders by collecting and sharing online the latest statistics, research, and treatment and recovery information.

As you read, consider the following questions:

1. According to ANRED, how do brain chemistry and starving-and-binging behaviors form a vicious cycle in the development of eating disorders?

2. What psychological factors increase the risk of developing an eating disorder, according to ANRED?

3. According to the author, how do differences in the way men and women are portrayed in the media explain why so many more women than men develop eating disorders?

There are many theories, many interwoven factors, and no one simple answer that covers persons with an eating disorder. For any particular individual, some or all of the following factors will combine to produce starving, stuffing, and purging.

Biological Factors

According to recent research (*Archives of General Psychiatry* 2006; 63:305–312) genetic factors account for more than half (56 percent) of the risk of developing anorexia nervosa. Work on the genetics of bulimia and binge eating continues.

Temperament seems to be, at least in part, genetically determined. Some personality types (obsessive-compulsive and sensitive-avoidant, for example) are more vulnerable to eating disorders than others. New research suggests that genetic factors predispose some people to anxiety, perfectionism, and obsessive-compulsive thoughts and behaviors. These people seem to have more than their share of eating disorders. In fact, people with a mother or sister who has had anorexia nervosa are 12 times more likely than others with no family history of that disorder to develop it themselves. They are four times more likely to develop bulimia (*Eating Disorders Review*, Nov./Dec. 2002).

Studies reported in the *New England Journal of Medicine* indicate that for some, but not all, people, heredity is an important factor in the development of obesity and binge eating. Now there are suggestions that women who develop anorexia nervosa have excess activity in the brain's dopamine receptors, which regulate pleasure. This may lead to an explanation of why they feel driven to lose weight but receive no pleasure from shedding pounds (*Journal of Biological Psychiatry*, July 2005. Guido Frank, et al.).

Also, once a person begins to starve, stuff, or purge, those behaviors in and of themselves can alter brain chemistry and prolong the disorder. For example, both undereating and over-eating can activate brain chemicals that produce feelings of peace and euphoria, thus temporarily dispelling anxiety and depression. In fact some researchers believe that eating-disordered folks may be using food to self-medicate painful feelings and distressing moods.

A note about stress and overeating: New research suggests that there is a biological link between stress and the drive to eat. Comfort foods—high in sugar, fat, and calories—seem to calm the body's response to chronic stress. In addition, hor-mones produced when one is under stress encourage the for-mation of fat cells. In Westernized countries life tends to be competitive, fast paced, demanding, and stressful. There may be a link between so-called modern life and increasing rates of overeating, overweight, and obesity. (Study to be published in Proceedings of the National Academy of Sciences. Author is Mary Dallman, professor of physiology, University of Califor-nia at San Francisco [2003].)

Age and brain maturation/impairment play a role also. When an eating disorder begins in childhood or adolescence, it may be especially hard to deal with. Magnetic resonance imaging provides evidence the brain continues to develop and become increasingly complex until people are in their early 20s. The parts of the brain that effectively plan ahead, predict consequences, and manage emotional impulses are just not fully operational in children and teens. Teens may insist they are mature, but the research shows there's a lot more brain wiring that needs to be done before the he or she is truly an adult (David Walsh, *Why Do They Act That Way?* Free Press, Simon & Schuster, 2004.).

And if that were not enough, even when the person is well past 20, starvation, chronic dieting, binge eating and purging can upset brain wiring and chemistry, impairing the very centers needed to make healthy choices.

Psychological Factors

People with eating disorders tend to be perfectionistic. They have unrealistic expectations of themselves and others. In spite of their many achievements, they feel inadequate and defective. In addition, they see the world as black and white, no shades of gray. Everything is either good or bad, a success or a failure, fat or thin. If fat is bad and thin is good, then thinner is better, and thinnest is best—even if thinnest is sixty-eight pounds [31 kg] in a hospital bed on life support.

Some people with eating disorders use the behaviors to avoid sexuality. Others use them to try to take control of themselves and their lives. They want to be in control and in charge. They are strong, usually winning the power struggles they find themselves in, but inside they feel weak, powerless, victimized, defeated, and resentful.

People with eating disorders often lack a sense of identity. They try to define themselves by manufacturing a socially approved and admired exterior. They have answered the existential question, "Who am I?" by symbolically saying "I am, or I am trying to be, thin. Therefore, I matter."

People with eating disorders often are legitimately angry, but because they seek approval and fear criticism, they do not dare express that anger directly. They do not know how to express it in healthy ways. They turn it against themselves by starving or stuffing.

It is often said that the key to understanding an eating disorder is an appreciation of the person's need to control—everything: life, schedules, friends, family, food, and especially one's own body. That is true, but there is another factor at least equally important: aspiration to perfection. When people embark on a weight loss program with all the fervor of a pilgrim seeking holiness, it becomes evident that they are hoping for and working to achieve a magical conversion process. By losing weight, they hope to transform their dull caterpillar selves into beautiful butterflies that lead lives of contentment, happiness, confidence and completion. How sad. If losing weight truly did lead to happiness, we would be a planet of bean poles.

Happiness, of course, is attainable, but through meaningful work, nourishing relationships, and a connection to something greater than oneself. Magical thinking and simplistic self-improvement programs just aren't up to the challenge.

Family Factors

Some people with eating disorders say they feel smothered in overprotective families. Others feel abandoned, misunderstood, and alone. Parents who overvalue physical appearance can unwittingly contribute to an eating disorder. So can those who make critical comments, even in jest, about their children's bodies.

Families that include a person with an eating disorder tend to be overprotective, rigid, and ineffective at resolving conflict. Sometimes mothers are emotionally cool while fathers are physically or emotionally absent. At the same time, there are high expectations of achievement and success. Children learn not to disclose doubts, fears, anxieties, and imperfections. Instead they try to solve their problems by manipulating weight and food, trying to achieve the appearance of success even if they do not feel successful.

Research at Oregon Health and Science University in Portland has produced strong evidence that exposure to stress (abuse, neglect, loss of a parent) in childhood increases the risk of behavioral and emotional problems (anxiety, depression, suicidality, drug abuse—phenomena frequently associated with eating disorders) in teenagers and young adults.

In addition, other research suggests that daughters of mothers with histories of eating disorders may be at higher risk of eating disorders themselves than are children of mothers with few food and weight issues. Children learn attitudes about dieting and their bodies through observation. When mom is dissatisfied with her body and frequently diets, daughters will learn to base their self-worth on their appearance, says Christine Gerbstadt, spokeswoman for the American Dietetic Association.

Alison Field, lead author of a Harvard study of peer, parent and media influences on children's dieting behavior and body image attutudes (*Pediatrics*, vol. 107, no. 1, January 2001, pp. 54–60) adds that "even small cues—such as making self-deprecating remarks about bulging thighs or squealing in delight over a few lost pounds—can send the message that thinness is to be prized above all else."

According to a report published in the April 1999 issue of the *International Journal of Eating Disorders*, mothers who have anorexia, bulimia, or binge eating disorder handle food issues and weight concerns differently than mothers who have never had eating disorders.

Patterns are observable even in infancy. They include odd feeding schedules, using food for rewards, punishments, comfort, or other non-nutritive purposes, and concerns about their daughters' weight.

Still to be determined is whether or not daughters of mothers with eating disorders will themselves become eating disordered when they reach adolescence.

Also, if mothers and fathers preach and nag about junk food and try to limit their children's access to treats, the children will desire and overeat these very items. A recent study (*American Journal of Clinical Nutrition*, 2003, 78:215) indicates that when parents restrict eating, children are more likely to eat when they are not hungry. The more severe the restriction,

Eating Disorders Defy Simple Explanations

Simply put, there is no single cause for an eating disorder. They are complex illnesses with multiple causes that require treatment across a number of domains. Eating disorders are better considered as "developmental" rather than "mental" problems. This acknowledges the depth and breadth of systems that are affected, and minimizes the stigma still associated with psychological disorders. . . .

1) Eating disorders are serious and complex problems that should not be simplified as "anorexia is just a plea for attention," or "bulimia is just an addiction to food." Eating disorders arise from a variety of physical, emotional, social, and familial issues, all of which need to be addressed for effective prevention and treatment; 2) eating disorders should not be framed as a "woman's problem" or "something for the girls."

Richard E. Kreipe, "Eating Disorders and Adolescents,"
Research Facts and Findings, *Cornell University ACT for Youth Center of Excellence, November 2006.*
www.actforyouth.net.

the stronger the desire to eat prohibited foods. These behaviors may set the stage for a full blown eating disorder in the future.

Social Factors

Sometimes appearance-obsessed friends or romantic partners create pressure that encourages eating disorders. Ditto for sorority houses, theatre troupes, dance companies, school cliques, and other situations where peers influence one another in unhealthy ways.

People vulnerable to eating disorders, in most cases, are experiencing relationship problems, loneliness in particular. Some may be withdrawn with only superficial or conflicted connections to other people. Others may seem to be living exciting lives filled with friends and social activities, but later they will confess that they did not feel they really fit in, that no one seemed to really understand them, and that they had no true friends or confidants with whom they could share thoughts, feelings, doubts, insecurities, fears, hopes, ambitions, and so forth—the basis of true intimacy. Often they desperately want healthy connections to others but fear criticism and rejection if their perceived flaws and shortcomings become known.

Cultural Pressures

In Westernized countries characterized by competitive striving for success, and in pockets of affluence in developing countries, women often experience unrealistic cultural demands for thinness. They respond by linking self-esteem to weight.

Cultural expectations can be cruel and unrelenting. "In order for a woman to consider herself happy, she has to be in a good relationship, be happy with her kids, her friends have to like her, her job has to be going well, her house has to look really good—and she has to be thin" (Professor Alice Domar, Harvard Medical School, *Parade* magazine, October 11, 2003).

Media Factors

Quote: Advertising has done more to cause the social unrest of the 20th century than any other single factor. —Clare Boothe Luce, American author and diplomat (1903-1987)

People in Western countries are flooded by media words and images. An average U.S. child, for example, sees more than 30,000 TV commercials each year (TV-Turnoff Network, 2005). That child sees more than 21 hours of TV each week plus dozens of magazines and many movies every year. In those media, happy and successful people are almost always portrayed by actors and models who are young, toned, and thin. The vast majority are stylishly dressed and have spent much time on hair styles and makeup.

> Factoid: According to *Health* magazine, April 2002, 32% of female TV network characters are underweight, while only 5% of females in the U.S. audience are underweight.

In contrast, evil, stupid, or buffoonish people are portrayed by actors who are older, frumpier, unkempt, perhaps physically challenged. Many are fat.

> Factoid: Again according to *Health* magazine, only 3% of female TV network characters are obese, while 25% of U.S. women fall into that category.

Most people want to be happy and successful, states that require thought, personal development, and usually hard work. The media, especially ads and commercials for appearance-related items, suggest that we can avoid the hard character work by making our bodies into copies of the icons of success.

Reading between the lines of many ads reveals a not-so-subtle message—"You are not acceptable the way you are. The only way you can become acceptable is to buy our product and try to look like our model (who is six feet tall [1.8 m] and wears size four jeans—and is probably anorexic). If you can't quite manage it, better keep buying our product. It's your only hope."

The differences between media images of happy, successful men and women are interesting. The women, with few exceptions, are young and thin. Thin is desirable. The men are young or older, but the heroes and good guys are strong and powerful in all the areas that matter—physically, in the business world, and socially. For men in the media, thin is not desirable; power, strength and competency are desirable. Thin men are seen as skinny, and skinny men are often depicted as sick, weak, frail, or deviant.

These differences are reflected in male and female approaches to self-help. When a man wants to improve himself, he often begins by lifting weights to become bigger, stronger, and more powerful. When a woman wants to improve herself, she usually begins with a diet, which will leave her smaller, weaker, and less powerful. Yet females have just as strong needs for power and control as do males.

Many people believe this media stereotyping helps explain why about ninety percent of people with eating disorders are women and only ten percent are men.

In recent years it has become politically correct for the media to make some effort to combat eating disorders. We have seen magazine articles and TV shows featuring the perils and heartbreak of anorexia and bulimia, but these efforts seem weak and ineffective when they are presented in the usual context. For example, how can one believe that a fashion magazine is truly motivated to combat anorexia when their articles about that subject are surrounded by advertisements featuring anorexic-looking models? How can one believe that the talk show hostess is truly in favor of strong, healthy female bodies when she frequently prods her stick-like thighs and talks about how much she wants to lose weight from her already scrawny body?

In May 1999, research was published that demonstrated the media's unhealthy affect on women's self-esteem and body awareness. In 1995, before television came to their island, the people of Fiji thought the ideal body was round, plump, and soft. Then, after 38 months of *Melrose Place, Beverly Hills 90210,* and similar western shows, Fijian teenage girls showed serious signs of eating disorders.

In another study, females who regularly watch TV three or more nights per week are fifty percent more likely than non-watchers to feel "too big" or "too fat." About two-thirds of the TV-watching female teens dieted in the month preceding the survey. Fifteen percent admitted vomiting to control their weight. TV shows like the two mentioned above are fantasies, but all over the world young women, and some not so young, accept them as instructions on how to look and act. That's really a shame.

An important question for people who watch TV, read magazines, and go to movies—do these media present images that open a window on the real world, or do they hold up a fun-house mirror in which the reflections of real people are distorted into impossibly tall, thin sticks (or impossibly muscular, steroid-dependent male action figures)? Media consumers need to be wise consumers of visual images.

For more information on this topic, we recommend *Remote Control Childhood? Combatting the Hazards of Media Culture*, a book by Diane Levin. In addition, parents can help their children learn to think critically by teaching them to ask the following questions about material presented through the media:

- Who created the message?

- For what purpose? (It's often to sell something. Sitcoms, for example, are considered "bait" by the TV industry to attract viewers who can then be shown commercials.)

- Does the message make me want something? Who benefits if I do want this thing and pay to get it?

- Is the message accurate or true?

- What lifestyles and values are presented? Which ones are omitted?

- Who are the so-called experts? Paid actors or real people?

- If research is cited, is it real science or just surveys and anecdotes?

Triggers

If people are vulnerable to eating disorders, sometimes all it takes to put the ball in motion is a trigger event that they do not know how to handle. A trigger could be something as seemingly innocuous as teasing or as devastating as rape or incest.

Triggers often happen at times of transition, shock, or loss where increased demands are made on people who already are unsure of their ability to meet expectations. Such triggers might include puberty, starting a new school, beginning a new job, death, divorce, marriage, family problems, breakup of an important relationship, critical comments from someone important, graduation into a chaotic, competitive world, and so forth.

There is some evidence to suggest that girls who achieve sexual maturity ahead of peers, with the associated development of breasts, hips, and other physical signs of womanhood, are at increased risk of becoming eating disordered. They may wrongly interpret their new curves as "being fat" and feel uncomfortable because they no longer look like peers who still have childish bodies.

Wanting to take control and fix things, but not really knowing how, and under the influence of a culture that equates success and happiness with thinness, the person tackles her/his body instead of the problem at hand. Dieting, bingeing, purging, exercising, and other strange behaviors are not random craziness. They are heroic, but misguided and ineffective, attempts to take charge in a world that seems overwhelming.

Sometimes people with medical problems such as diabetes, people who must pay meticulous attention to what they eat, become vulnerable to eating disorders. A certain amount of obsessiveness is necessary for health, but when the fine line is crossed, healthy obsessiveness can quickly become pathological.

Perhaps the most common trigger of disordered eating is dieting. It is a bit simplistic, but nonetheless true, to say that if there were no dieting, there would be no anorexia nervosa. Neither would there be the bulimia that people create when they diet, make themselves chronically hungry, overeat in response to hunger pangs and cravings, and then, panicky about weight gain, vomit or otherwise purge to get rid of the calories.

Feeling guilty and perhaps horrified at what they have done, they swear to "be good." That usually means more dieting, which leads to more hunger, and so the cycle repeats again and again. It is axiomatic in eating disorders treatment programs that the best way to avoid a binge is to never, ever allow oneself to become ravenously hungry. It is far wiser to be aware of internal signals and respond to hunger cues early on by eating appropriate amounts of nourishing, healthy food.

Multidimensional Risk Factors

A panel at the 2004 International Conference on Eating Disorders in Orlando, Florida, suggested the following spectrum of risk factors. The more any one person has, the greater the probability of developing an eating disorder.

- High weight concerns before age 14

- High level of perceived stress

- Behavior problems before age 14

- History of dieting

- Mother diets and is concerned about appearance

- Siblings diet and are concerned about appearance

- Peers diet and are concerned about appearance

- Negative self-evaluation

- Perfectionism

- No male friends

- Parental control

- Rivalry with one or more siblings

- Competitive with siblings' shape and/or appearance

- Shy and/or anxious

- Distressed by parental arguments

- Distressed by life events occurring in the year before the illness develops

- Critical comments from family members about weight, shape and eating

- Teasing about weight, shape and appearance

> "It's not just anorexics who pedestal the thin; we all do. . . . After all, the mantra of our age is that thin gets you noticed."

Cultural Obsession with Thinness Is Harmful

Mimi Spencer

In the following viewpoint, British columnist Mimi Spencer cites a pervasive cultural shift over the past twenty years—idealization of progressively thinner female bodies, to the point of emaciation—as a major reason for the rise in eating disorders in modern Western society. Ultrathinness alone now brings celebrity, Spencer argues; girls and women are bombarded with images of skinny show business and fashion icons in contexts that present thinness as desirable, and willingly starve themselves even when they know there is no healthy way to look like that. Mimi Spencer writes about popular culture for London's Guardian, Mail, *and* Observer *and* Harper's Bazaar.

As you read, consider the following questions:

1. According to Spencer, the average model weighed how much less than the average American woman in 1981? how much less in 2006?

2. As cited by Spencer, how does psychologist Andrew Hill explain thinness as a sign of status and character in Western society?

3. How has intense media involvement in celebrities' lives made ordinary people hypercritical of their own appearance, in the author's view?

She's far too thin. Everybody says so. In those shrunken hot pants and skinny red vest she looked positively ravenous, like an urchin from Oliver Twist—albeit one with this season's Prada handbag and hair extensions.

But just how skinny is Victoria Beckham? How would it feel if she sat on your lap? Would she be heavier than a kitten? If you hugged her would she break? We do know that she wears jeans with a minuscule 23-inch waist—the size, apparently, of a seven-year-old child (it is also, as it happens, the precise circumference of my head).

VB is not alone, of course, but merely the leading exponent of a New Look which has come to dominate our lives. Other exemplars include Lindsay Lohan, Mischa Barton, Nicole Richie, Kate Bosworth, Amy Winehouse—women relatively new on the celebrity radar who skitter across the pages of magazines, coat hangers furnished with tennis-ball boobs and expensive shoes, not a shred of fat to share among them. You might not give a tossed salad how much these bony birds weigh. You might even agree with Kate Hudson (who recently won a libel action against the UK *National Enquirer* magazine for implying she had an eating disorder) that it is none of our business. But it is. It matters because hyper-thin has somehow become today's celebrity standard and, as a result—almost without us noticing—the goalposts have moved for us all.

With every image of Nicole Richie's feeble wrists or Posh Spice's concave thighs—which seem to shy away from each other as if they've never been properly introduced—with every shot, an inch or an ounce is shaved off the notional ideal female form which governs our relationship with our bodies and with the world. Images of Lindsay Lohan's chest bones, desperately reaching out to greet strangers, or Keira Knightley's xylophone of vertebrae, countable at 30 paces, have burned themselves into our consciousness so that uber-thin no longer looks odd. It no longer shocks. But it does make you look at your own soft, warm body in a hard new light. It's almost as if, in the course of a generation, we've overturned the age-old feminine ideal—maternal, curvaceous, zaftig.

Looking now at pictures of Linda Evangelista in her super-model prime, or Elizabeth Hurley in her safety-pin Versace frock, they look—unbelievably—a bit on the heavy side, even though at the time they seemed radiantly slim. To achieve this mental switcheroo, something seismic has happened, enough to make a body mass index of 10 (the BMA [British Medical Association] recommends something in the region of 22) look nearly normal to our rewired brains. When you rub your eyes, though, and snap yourself out of the reverie, you realise that this isn't glamorous. It's cadaverously, dangerously thin.

I have seen this kind of thin before. It resided in the endocrinology department at the Royal Free Hospital in Hampstead, where a member of my own family was treated for anorexia throughout her teens. Little could I have known that, in the intervening two decades, the morbidly hungry body type I saw there would become celebrated, a glory to which women of all ages might aspire.

And they do. We do. If we are truthful, it's not just anorexics who pedestal the thin; we all do, to one extent or another. After all, the mantra of our age is that thin gets you noticed. It gets you a contract as a TV presenter or a model or a singer in a girl band. Thin fast-tracks you with far more alacrity than a degree in history. More than that, as a society, we tend to cast a forgiving eye upon the very thin, while castigating the repugnantly fat.

Here on my desk, I have a copy of *TeenNow* magazine, a junior version of the best-selling gossip title. 'What Celebrities Really Weigh' is its scream-green cover-line. Victoria Beckham, FYI, weighs 7st 10lb [108 lb]; Lindsay Lohan is 7st 8lb [106 lb]; Hilary Duff weighs in at 7st 7lb [105 lb], the same as Nadine Coyle from Girls Aloud ('My legs are always going to be skinny,' she says. 'There's nothing I can do about that.' Oh yes there is, Nadine! Try chocolate fudge cake. Works for me every time.)

Mischa Barton, meanwhile, is 7st 5lb [103 lb]. Even Katie Price, with her heavyweight frontage, only tips the scales at eight stone [112 lb]. Nicole Richie, though, is the runt in the bunch, weighing a painful 6st 9lb [93 lb]. 'I know I'm too thin,' she is quoted as saying. 'I wouldn't want any young girl looking at me wanting to be like me. I'm not happy with the way I look right now.'

Why then are *TeenNow* readers getting a Technicolor gawp at her? She's not there, surely, as a warning, but as a temptation. Editor Jeremy Mark seems affronted by the suggestion. 'When we do weight covers, we are scrupulously careful not to suggest that skinniness should be an aim for our readers; we always offer professional advice about healthy eating. It's a touchy subject, particularly among teens, so everything is checked by lawyers and doctors. We certainly have a responsibility to show balance in the images that we choose—which is why we also show Charlotte Church, Joss Stone, Kelly Clarkson, Scarlett Johansson, Beyoncé or Colleen—women with a more rounded shape as a reassurance to our readers.'

Come on, Jeremy, I say. You know thin sells. That's why *Heat* magazine ran 'She's sooo Skinny!' cover lines for a dozen consecutive weeks and smashed their sales figures in the process. Mark eventually concedes that, 'Yes, it's a common belief that you must be thin to be beautiful; there's so much pressure on celebrities to look that way. It's all about ad deals, sponsorship, winning contracts. Pepsi aren't going to book you if you're a size 16, are they? They'll book Cheryl Tweedy instead.'

At the Rhodes Farm Clinic for Eating Disorders in north London, Dr Dee Dawson has noticed a startling jump in the numbers of very young children suffering from anorexia and bulimia. 'We see lots of 10-year-olds,' she says with a sigh. 'The link with celebrity cannot be overstated; though anorexics talk of family problems, the pressure of school or not wanting to grow up, we're now seeing girls who openly say they want to look like Victoria Beckham. Thinness is valued. Among my patients, she is one of the top icons: as far as they can see, she gets invited everywhere, she's got plenty of money, a handsome husband. It's not surprising that they associate her body shape with glamour and success.'

ChildLine too reports an increased number of calls from children, some as young as 10, seeking help with eating disorders. The figure rose from 1,000 in 2001 to 1,500 [in 2005]. In a culture which venerates thin, ChildLine reports that it's not unusual for children as young as seven to believe they are fat. Here's a chat-room post from Rachael, age 12:

> I have always hated the way I look. I try to look in the mirror as little as possible. I am curvy in all the wrong places, and if I see someone really slim and pretty it makes me want to cry. But seeing all of the celebs in tight skinny outfits does make me want to lose weight! I've done it before and I'm going to do it again!

In the darker recesses of the internet, where teenagers increasingly reside, Victoria Beckham has become a macabre pin-up among subscribers to the web's many pro-ana websites. Here, anorexics exchange tips on how to starve themselves effectively ('Smoking burns calories,' offers one contributor; 'If your stomach grumbles, hit it,' suggests another),

Cultural Obsession with Body Image Promotes Male Eating Disorders

We are constantly bombarded with images of the perfect body, the ideal body, and the most beautiful form. We as a society rarely stop to think about the effects of unrealistically toned models and bodybuilders, or the value we place upon strength, has on our men.

Wayne State University counselor Dr. Galen Duncan said, "In the media, the most successful ones are those incredibly well-built individuals."

For men, the pressure to be attractive to others and to meet impossible standards set forth by our image-obsessed society can have severely damaging effects.

They may spend hours in the gym, eat too little for proper nutrition or eat massive amounts of unhealthy foods, all in an effort to meet their expected potentials.

According to the Boston College Eating Awareness Team, "One to five percent of all men have seriously unhealthy eating behaviors that would qualify as eating disorders. Ten to 15 percent of people with eating disorders are male."

Alicia Chmielewski, "Male Eating Disorders: The Truth About Body Image," The South End, Wayne State University, October 4, 2004.

together with 'thinspirational' images of their favourite celebrities. 'I envy her thin legs and chest,' writes one Posh fan. 'She has beautiful bones sticking out of her chest.'

Beautiful bones? Hardly, says Dr Dee Dawson. 'With a body like that, she'll be osteoporotic very early, she's unlikely to be menstruating, her muscles are being eaten from within—even her heart will have wasted away.' Furthermore, what these girls are admiring is something that doesn't exist in nature—a random handful of body parts held together with eye-lash glue. Says Dawson, with unapologetic ire, 'You can count every single one of her ribs, and then you come to those domes of bosoms that there's no way she could produce herself. If she had the right breasts to go with that frame, she'd have nipples and nothing else!'

Yet that weightless, curiously proportioned body is idolised—by all of us, whether we should know better or not. Look at Nicole Kidman, Jennifer Aniston, Keira Knightley, Christina Ricci, Teri Hatcher, Eva Herzigova, any model on any catwalk anywhere in the world—I've got handbags that weigh more than they do. I could fold Eva Longoria up and pop her in my pocket. In this looking-glass world, a 100-pounder [7 stone] is a heavyweight. Size 00—a logical impossibility when you pause to consider it—is now Hollywood's dress-size of choice. True perspective can be gained when you consider that the pin-up of the 1890s was Lillian Russell, all 200 pounds [14 stone] of her. We don't even have to mention Jayne Mansfield, Marilyn Monroe, Sophia Loren—none of whom would get the job today—to know that something's up. Studies have shown that, while 25 years ago the average model weighed eight per cent less than the average American woman (and, yes, Twiggy was abnormally petite in her day), today's model weighs 23 per cent below the national average. This points up the fascinating paradox that, while we are desperate to keep up with our ever-shrinking celebrities, the average woman is actually getting bulkier. We're round like melons and fat like sausages, despite obsessing about our lardy arses every day. Fat lot of good it does us. While our icons are running the distinct risk of slipping between the cracks in the pavement, we're turning into bollards [thick posts]. Thirty-eight per cent of British women are now classified as overweight, and one in five is obese. If we resemble anyone, it's not Posh Spice. It's Elton John.

As long ago as 2000, the BMA, in its report 'Eating Disorders, Body Image and the Media', noted that the extreme thinness of celebrities was 'both unachievable and biologically inappropriate', observing that the gap between the media ideal and the reality appeared to be making eating disorders worse. 'At present, certain sections of the media provide images of extremely thin or underweight women in contexts which suggest that these weights are healthy or desirable,' it stated, recommending that normal women in the upper reaches of a healthy weight should be 'more in evidence on television as role models for young women'. Television producers and those in advertising should review their employment of very thin women, and the Independent Television Commission should review its advertising policy, the report recommended. Six years on, the converse has happened.

To maintain their 'biologically inappropriate' body shape, our celebrities—those brave enough to step up to the plate and admit it—are permanently hungry. Elizabeth Hurley has confessed as much. Marcia Cross, who plays Bree in *Desperate Housewives*, recently admitted that staying thin was 'a living hell', and that she felt she had been banned from eating since joining the show. Actresses, models, singers, presenters—all are subject to the tyranny of thin enforced by the minders, moulders and producers who know very well what sells. . . . I know that it happens to hopeful young girls from the moment that first crumby Polaroid is taken in the reception of the modelling agency. Myleene Klass, a winner of the Popstars talent contest, was a size 12/14 until her then record company advised her to watch herself on video to see how fat she was. She was assigned a personal trainer, and told to become a size eight. Fast.

For years now the dreaded 'thin issue' has plagued the fashion press, who stand accused of promoting a singular and unachievable body shape with every androgynous little sparrow to grace their glossy pages. Every now and then, we see a

111

flutter of concern—when Omega pulled its ads from *Vogue* in a 1997 protest, for instance, or when the industry's prime movers were called to a meeting at Downing Street in 2000 to grapple with the issue. What tends to emerge after the dust has died down is a whole lot of nothing. There are occasional forays into the fat zone—a 1997 Nick Knight shoot in *Vogue* called 'Modern Curves' featured plus-size model Sara Morrison; in the same year, The Body Shop ran a series of ads with the tag line, 'There are three billion women who don't look like supermodels, and only eight who do'. Set against the vast portfolio of 'thimages' which make up the wallpaper of our lives, these trifling efforts have about as much impact as a bubble on the wind.

As Dr Dee Dawson notes, 'I've sat on endless discussion groups and panels with magazine editors, and they always say they're trying for balance, that they're going to change. It never happens.'

It did happen, once at least in my experience. When I worked at *Vogue* a decade ago, one of the editors produced a beach-shoot featuring a size-14 model. When they arrived in the office, the photos looked great; the model was statuesque, not overweight. But later, on the published page, tucked in between other shoots and ads featuring the starving Barbaras that are the usual glossy fodder, this lovely woman looked huge, as if she'd been inflated with a bicycle pump. No wonder the experiment wasn't repeated. . . . Given the choice, we'll take thin, thanks.

Following the Downing Street Initiative, Premier, a top model agency, argued convincingly that women who bought fashion magazines were as much to blame as the editors and advertisers who used them. 'It is a supply-and-demand thing—advertisers, magazines and agencies supply the image that consumers want to see. Statistics show that if you stick a beautiful skinny girl on the cover of a magazine you sell more copies.'

Vogue's editor Alexandra Shulman might well agree, though she's too polite to say so. Until lately, she has rather shirked the issue by saying, 'All we are doing is showing images of women we regard as interesting or beautiful or fashionable. But we are not actually saying you have to be like this.' [In 2005], though, Shulman was more candid. 'I really wish that models were a bit bigger because then I wouldn't have to deal with this the whole time,' she said in one newspaper interview. 'There is pressure on them to stay thin, and I'm always talking to the designers about it, asking why they can't just be a bit closer to a real woman's physique in terms of their ideal, but they're not going to do it. Clothes look better to all of our eyes on people who are thinner.'

Boom. The bottom line. Clothes. Put bluntly, clothes look better on a slim frame. 'Being skinny doesn't mean you've automatically got a good body, not at all,' confides one wafer-thin friend. 'Thin definitely doesn't give you good legs, just thinner legs. But it does, by and large, mean you'll look all right in clothes.'

And don't we all of us want that? In my experience, there's a constant jockeying for position on the weight front among women, a competitive, low-grade bitchery (rarely expressed, but captured, often, on the cover of *heat* or *Now*) which reveres the dropping of a dress size and stigmatises the gaining of a kilo. Of course, if you're bright and grown-up and plugged into the issues of the day, you tend not to let on that you're fascinated by other women's bottoms. But you are. We are. We look. We compare. In our image-saturated, overweight universe, we're hypercritical of our peers and our paragons. It's nothing to do with men (heaven knows, few men actually fancy the perilously thin females glorified by women; most would swap five Posh Spices for a Jennifer Lopez any day), and everything to do with competition between females.

'Women are duplicitous on this issue,' says Leeds Medical School psychologist Dr Andrew Hill. 'Much of the pressure about appearance and weight is applied by other women. In the face of nutritional abundance, women are showing their status by eating poorly—much as a corpulent belly historically indicated status in times of privation. It's perverse, but a reverse snobbery now informs our relationship with weight; being thin in an overeating society is a sign of control. It takes enormous will to stay so thin.

'Nationally, we're getting fatter by a percentage point each year—so people who are trying to lose weight, which means most of us, are in awe of the high achievers in the field. We're also intimately involved in celebrity lives in a way we never used to be. We're encouraged to have an opinion by an invasive media.'

The web makes it easier still. [In 2005] FeedLindsay.com amassed more than 30,000 signatures petitioning scrappy little Lohan to gain weight. [In February 2006] Nicole Richie was weighed 'live' on the prime-time *Howard Stern Show*, a grotesque freak fair for the modern age. (Since you ask, she was 92 pounds [6.5 stone], though observers speculate that she has slimmed down since then; besides, she was wearing jewellery at the time.)

With every diet tip and photo shoot offered by the famous, the more we are invited to take a seat at their table and judge and, says Dr Hill, the more self-critical we become as a society. As a result, he says, 'Weight control has become the ambition of a generation.'

For all but the very disciplined—or very disturbed—the kind of hyper-thin portrayed by the stars is an impossible goal, which is why so many Western women are in a constant state of food anxiety. Four in 10 of us are on a permanent diet. Ninety-eight per cent of us hate our bodies. We nurse our own little rituals, weight-management tics that were once the preserve of the Hurleys and Paltrows of this world, carefully tailored to suit our needs. We know how much bread we ate for lunch and whether we can, therefore, have half a potato for supper. We're living under a siege of our own making, bedevilled by a sickening guilt as we lick the last chocolate smear from a Magnum lolly.

Some, of course, are more passionate in their pursuit of thin than others. My wafer-thin friend is adamant that she is well within the bell-curve of normal when she describes her 'couture-eating disorder' thus: 'It may vary from writing down fat grams and cals consumed in a single day on the backs of envelopes, which is done as thoughtlessly as doodling, to the constant bits of fat-avoiding snippets we exchange, to 'snacking' on coffee because it takes the edge off hunger to having a glass of water or Diet Coke very close to hand if you ever decide to have a teeny bit of chocolate, so that you can wash away the taste immediately and stop yourself wanting more . . .' And this from an intelligent individual, who knows very well that the game of Thin Quest is the last word in banal. So, why? Why, after emancipation, feminism, after—ha ha—Girl Power—should pouring yourself into a very small frock be such a stellar achievement? Isn't it embarrassingly shallow and meaningless?

We persist, says Dr Hill, because weight has come to signify all that is desirable, because 'judgment of character is increasingly based on superficial appearance. We objectify celebrities, inferring all sorts of things from their physical appearance. Image colours everything, simply because, in a world overloaded with information, we cling to what is most obvious: and that's how things look.'

The recent influx of what Dr Hill calls 'talentless self-seeking bimbettes' into the fame game has only concentrated attention more fully on looks alone; that's all that remains now that silly old talent appears to have been excised from the equation. In Victoria Beckham's case, her 'thimage' has become a life raft for a sinking career. As one of her friends pointed out recently, 'Her figure is her career and with the spotlight constantly on her, she says she has to watch her weight very carefully. She doesn't care if some people think she's gone too far.'

If anything, she has come out fighting: 'I haven't got an eating disorder,' she snapped the other day, 'I'm just disciplined about what I eat.' But my, what discipline! Really, it's hard not to be impressed. Most of us would buckle after 10 minutes on her punishing regime. She chews for ages. She quizzes waiters to have them remove butter, oil and salad dressings from her plate. She doesn't eat portions that can't fit into the palm of her hand, 'as that's the same size as her stomach'. She only eats fruit till 3pm and then limits her intake to 500 calories for the rest of the day.

It's possible—as Dr Dee Dawson points out—that Posh doesn't have an eating disorder in the medical sense; anorexia and bulimia are, after all, psychiatric conditions characterised by a host of pathological behaviours and beliefs way beyond the normal range. While she displays plenty of these, she also has enough control and awareness to calibrate her food intake when she wants a child and then rein her appetite back in when she wants to dump the baby fat. According to the friend, 'Victoria knows that she'll have to start eating carbs if she has any hope of conceiving [a fourth baby].' Could you ask for a more revealing take on modern life?

While Victoria admits she has 'come close' to an eating disorder, other celebrities are more candid. Here's just a handful who have recently disclosed their own anorexia or bulimia (though they usually distance themselves from its grim reality by using the past tense): Mary Kate Olsen, Christina Ricci, Portia de Rossi, Calista Flockhart, Karen Elson, Tracy Shaw, Kate Beckinsale, Geri Halliwell, Melanie Chisholm. . . Not that it stops us wanting to look like them; we just choose to concentrate on their lovely slim arms and nutty buttocks rather than the fact that they have possibly just chucked up their lunch. Funny how a brain can curtain off unpalatable truths and feed happily on the garnish.

But perhaps we should look harder—at Victoria's sad little bod, at her desperate little jeans. Perhaps we should train ourselves to see the perma-hunger of the hyper-thin. Strip away the gloss, starve their lovely bones of the oxygen of publicity. In the final analysis, doesn't the responsibility lie not with them, but with us?

> *"Our culture is obsessed by thin. . . . And now I am, and I love it."*

Cultural Obsession with Thinness Is Not Harmful

Polly Vernon

In the following viewpoint, British style writer Polly Vernon disputes critics who charge society's emphasis on thinness is a harmful cause of eating disorders. Vernon writes from personal experience that since becoming thin she is envied by others who view her as more beautiful and more authoritative and she is both happier and less troubled by concerns over calories. Polly Vernon is a writer and editor for the London Observer *and a contributing editor for the weekly glossy magazine* Grazia.

As you read, consider the following questions:

1. How does Vernon explain her weight loss as natural and healthy?

2. In what ways does Vernon say as a thin person she is perceived differently by women and by men?

3. According to the author, how does being thin make her think less, not more, about food?

I didn't mean to get so thin. I liked food, especially super-market top-end ranges and expensive freebie work lunches. And I didn't have an eating disorder. Just the usual under-stated body image issues; that low-level discontent most women experience on watching the stars on a glossy Channel 4 American import go about their whip-thin, fragrant business. Aka Sex and the City syndrome.

But thin wasn't something I actively pursued. Thin hap-pened to me. Firstly, there was some heightened life turmoil. A new job, a very ill mother, general unease about where I was going now I had hit my thirties. None of which made me inclined to eat. Secondly, I became 'accidentally Atkins'. I fell spontaneously out of love with carbohydrates—with the pasta and bread that used to make up most of my meals—and in love with protein. I discovered fish, properly, for the first time ever. Sea bass, tuna steak, sword fish, yes!, went a bit yoghurt-based for breakfast, carpaccio of beef and rocket for lunch, fancy wilted spinach salad for dinner. In six months, I lost nearly two stone [28 lb]. On a clothes shopping expedition, I realised with vague interest that I'd gone from being a size 10 going on 12, to a size six going on eight. This tipped me and my five-five [165 cm] frame into the realm of what's techni-cally referred to as 'probably a bit too thin, lady'.

Thinness Changes People's Perceptions

What I didn't realise was how massively Thin would impact on my life. Beyond the predictable scenarios (mother fretting, lover wondering out loud if I was 'bulmenic' [sic]), other things changed. Rather excitingly, I was embraced by a fast and glam super-thin super-class. I was summoned for a drink by a group of women I used to work with on *Vogue*, a place where thinliness is not just next to godliness, it rates way, way above it. They practically applauded when I entered the bar. 'How did you do it?' asked the people who eat nothing (give or take the occasional pistachio nut—which, apparently, are

Cultural Ideals of Thinness Are Not to Blame for Eating Disorders

Many women criticize the media for glorifying certain unrealistic standards of beauty; however, due to the proliferation and popularity of fashion and beauty magazines, [Steven Thomsen writes] "seeing attractive models may become such a familiar experience that exposure no longer produces a reaction strong enough to influence self-perception or one's general sense of hope." Therefore exposure to these models is a lot less psychologically harmful than most would believe because women have become used to and desensitized to the imagery. [Marika Tiggermann and Belinda McGill note] that although "virtually all women and girls are exposed to a substantial dose of idealized thin beauty images, not all develop extreme preoccupation with weight, and only a minority develop clinically diagnosable eating disorders." It is impossible for American women to avoid images of women in the media; if body dissatisfaction and eating disorders were caused by the media, more women would be afflicted.

. . . [Nancy Etcoff writes], "one must keep in mind that ninety-eight percent of women do not develop diagnosable levels of eating disorders although all are exposed to the media." The role the media plays in creating a negative self-image for girls is, [Thomsen writes] "generally believed to be mediated by additional factors, including personality and temperament, emotional distress, endorsement of traditional gender roles, negative self-evaluation of achievement, teasing about appearance, low self-esteem, and body mass." The representation of thin women in the media doesn't cause these problems.

Gabrielle Berger, "Social Ideals of Beauty as Seen Through the Lens of the Media," Writing Seminar II: The Lure of Beauty, New York University, May 7, 2004. www.nyu.edu/gallatin/writing/pdf/BergerG.pdf.

the thin person's preferred bar snack because the time it takes to open them, multiplied by the possibility that you might break a nail on the shell, means you won't consume nearly as many as you might if they were, say, cashews). 'Stress, grief, a bit of abject misery, accidental Atkins,' I told them. 'Wow,' they said. 'Brilliant.'

We spent the night drinking cinnamon Bellinis, the Diet Coke of the cocktail world. We waved away the canapes on offer. We didn't eat: caramelised red onion and soured cream blinis, mini portions of sausage and mash on big china spoons, California rolls, mini lemon mousses in shot glasses. Everyone hung on my every word because I was newly, truly *thin*, and therefore authoritative.

Not everyone was so impressed. Old friends started watching me when we lunched together. I could see them thinking: why doesn't she have any bread? And why is she only having a starter? That's the oldest trick in the book, that is! They stealth-ordered extra portions of fat chips for me, in the vain hope I wouldn't notice. I did.

Men, in general, do not approve. Builders accost me on the street, telling me I could be a 'good-looking bird, if I ate a bit more'. They wave their sandwiches at me, in case I am a bit hazy on what food looks like. When I was loudly declaring my love of dark choc Baci in my local Italian deli, I heard the man in the queue behind me mutter, 'Yeah, right.' In short: you get thin, you become public property.

Thinness Changes My Perceptions of Myself

Our culture is obsessed by thin and by The Thin, by the obesity versus anorexia debate, by our (women's, obviously) constant taboo pursuit of thinness. A celebrity who isn't incredibly thin isn't generally considered 'A-list'. It's not right, but there it is. Everybody wants to be thinner. Whatever they say. And now I am, and I love it. I lost weight by accident, but I could have put it all back on again by now if I'd wanted to. But I don't.

Contrary to popular belief, being thin has made me happy. I've spent probably 16 years wondering if I would look better if I were skinnier, and now I know for sure. I do. But then almost everyone does. I like the way clothes fit me. And I like having cheekbones (although I admit I can look a touch gaunt in harsh lighting). As one of the most astute women I know said to me recently: 'You've lost too much weight. God, I love it when people say that to me.'

And weirdly, I like food more, now that I am untroubled by Sex and the City syndrome. I certainly think about it a lot less. I don't waste time calculating that day's fat intake, totting up calories consumed absent-mindedly on the corner of a Post-it. I don't need to. I know it's not that much: that's sushi for you.

My friends have re-christened me Thinny Girl, and I love it. Thin is part of who I am now and I thoroughly intend to make the best of it. With no apologies.

> *"The fashion industry, from designer to magazine editors, should not be making icons out of anorexically thin models."*

The Fashion Industry Promotes Eating Disorders

Janet Treasure et al.

In 2006 the organizers of the annual Cibeles Fashion Show in Madrid took the unprecedented step of banning significantly underweight models from participation, sparking international debate over whether the fashion industry's use of emaciated models encouraged anorexia and other eating disorders in the general population. Professor Janet Treasure and forty of her colleagues at the Eating Disorders Service and Research Unit (EDRU) at King's College, a well-known British eating disorders treatment clinic, applauded the Spanish authorities' decision. The following viewpoint is an open letter from the EDRU group to the international fashion industry urging similar actions to discourage the glamorization of anorexic imagery in the media and modern culture.

Janet Treasure and EDRU Team of King's College, London, open letter, "To the Fashion Industry as Represented by the British Fashion Council," October 4, 2006. Reproduced by permission of the author.

As you read, consider the following questions:

1. According to the authors, what critical effects do disrupted eating patterns have on physical development?

2. What percentage of models fell below the minimum weight for participation in the 2006 Madrid fashion show, according to Treasure and her colleagues?

3. According to the authors, what is the normal body mass index (BMI) range? the BMI cutoff for the Madrid fashion show? the BMI cutoff for clinical diagnosis of anorexia?

TO THE FASHION INDUSTRY AS REPRESENTED BY THE BRITISH FASHION COUNCIL

Eating disorders, anorexia nervosa and bulimia nervosa are common disorders found in nearly 10% of young women. There is a large range in clinical severity. Some cases are mild and transient. However in the clinic we see the dark side whereby the quality of life of the individual and her family shrivels away and the shadow of death looms. These disorders have the highest risk of physical and psychosocial morbidity than any other psychological condition. The costs for the individual, the family and society are huge. Therefore research has focused on trying to prevent these disorders and to identify the factors that cause or maintain them.

Anorexia nervosa has a long history but bulimia nervosa was rare in women born before the 1950's. The incidence of the binge eating disorders like that of obesity has rapidly increased in the last half of the twentieth century. Most experts agree that cultural factors in terms of eating behaviours and values about weight and shape are important causal and maintaining elements in the bingeing disorders. The internalisation of the thin ideal is a key risk factor. Dieting to attain this idealized form can trigger an erratic pattern of eating especially if it is used in combination with extreme behaviours that compensate for overeating.

The Fashion Industry Should Be Held Accountable

After years of promising to clean up its act voluntarily, the fashion industry [must] be forced into protecting both the health of the models it uses, and the impact their images can have on impressionable young girls and women.

Steve Bloomfield, of the Eating Disorders Association, said [in October 2006]: "We do think legislation is needed. The industry will not act voluntarily because the fashion world is so competitive and no-one wants to be the first to do anything in case they lose out.

"A law would create a level playing field. Agencies would not be able to hire models below a certain body mass index (BMI) and magazines and designers would not be able to use images of them.

"This is about protecting the young women and men who work in the fashion industry, as well as those who are at risk of an eating disorder, and can be influenced by the pictures that they see."

Maxine Frith, "You Can Never Be Too Thin—Or Can You?"
Babynet, October 12, 2006.

Studies in animals suggest that persistent, changes in the brain and behaviour like those seen in the addictions result if the pattern of eating is disrupted in critical developmental periods. The paradox can be that a desire to be thin can set in train a pattern of disturbed eating which increases the risk for obesity. So how can this society protect young people from these consequences? Interesting work in colleges in the USA reported this year has shown that an educational web based intervention promoting a healthy relationship with food and body image can prevent the onset of an eating disorder in those that are at highest risk. Such use of the web can act as an antidote to the pro-ana (pro-anorexia) web sites which foster toxic attitudes and unrealistic body forms.

Public health interventions may also be warranted. Spain has taken the first step. The Health Authorities of the Region of Madrid and the Annual Cibeles Fashion Show (Pasarela Cibeles) banned extremely thin models from participating in this year's event. Models with a Body Mass Index (BMI) below 18kg/m^2 (30% of the participants) were offered medical help rather than a position on the catwalk. To put this in context, the average BMI for a healthy woman is between 19 to 25kg/m^2. To be clearly diagnosed with anorexia nervosa a BMI of less than 17.5 is needed although in most treatment centres people with a higher BMI have levels of clinical severity that warrant treatment.

The issue is not whether we should place the blame of unhealthy eating behaviours on the Fashion Industry or on anyone else. The issue is that Spanish Health Authorities have decided to intervene in a health issue, which is directly affecting the well-being of models as well as affecting the attitudes and behaviours of many young girls and women who may strive to imitate and attain these unhealthy pursuits.

Adopting what Madrid has done is a good first step but the fashion industry, from designer to magazine editors, should not be making icons out of anorexically thin models. Magazines should stop printing these pictures and designers should stop designing for these models. People may say that clothes look better on skinny models but do not forget there was a time when smoking looked good too.

Janet Treasure and EDRU Team

> *"The notion that the fashion industry should endure government meddling because its products or marketing techniques may [promote] an unhealthy desire for thinness seems dubious at best."*

The Fashion Industry Should Not Be Held Responsible for Eating Disorders

Michelle Cottle

In the following viewpoint, Michelle Cottle argues that the fashion industry has no obligation to change its practices, including using ultra-skinny models. It is not in the business of promoting healthy body images, Cottle suggests, just as fast-food restaurants are not in the business of selling healthy food. Michelle Cottle is a senior editor at the New Republic.

As you read, consider the following questions:

1. To what other industries selling risky products, but nevertheless not subject to regulation, does Cottle compare the fashion industry?

Michelle Cottle, "Model Behavior," The *New Republic* online, September 15, 2006. www.tnr.com/doc.mhtml?i=w060911&s=cottle092506. Reproduced by permission of *The New Republic*.

2. What two criteria, in Cottle's view, *would* constitute grounds for intervention in the fashion industry?

3. What does the author say will eventually happen to resolve the issue of ultra-thin models on the catwalk?

Call it Revenge of the Carb Lovers. While much of the Middle East continues to devour itself, the hot controversy to come out of the West [in September 2006] is Madrid's decision to ban super-skinny models from its fashion week, the Pasarela Cibeles, which begins on September 18th. Responding to complaints from women's groups and health associations about the negative impact of emaciated models on the body image of young women, the Madrid regional government, which sponsors the Pasarela Cibeles, demanded that the show's organizers go with fuller-figured gals, asserting that the industry has a responsibility to portray healthy body images. As Concha Guerra, the deputy finance minister for the regional administration, eloquently put it, "Fashion is a mirror and many teenagers imitate what they see on the catwalk."

Activists' concerns are easy to understand. With ultra-thinness all the rage on the catwalk, your average model is about 5' 9" and 110 pounds [7.8 stone]. But henceforth, following the body mass index standard set by Madrid, a 5' 9" model must weigh at least 123 pounds [8.8 stone]. (To ensure there's no cheating, physicians will be on site to examine anyone looking suspiciously svelte.) Intrigued by the move, other venues are considering similar restrictions—notably the city of Milan, whose annual show is considerably more prestigious than Madrid's.

Industry Opposition

Modeling agencies meanwhile, are decidedly unamused. Cathy Gould of New York's Elite agency publicly denounced the ban as an attempt to scapegoat the fashion world for eating disorders—not to mention as gross discrimination against both

Banning Ultra-Thin Models Violates the Rights of Designers and Models

The policy [of banning ultra-thin models from fashion-show runways] is clearly an infringement on the free speech of fashion designers. Design is a form of expression and a fashion show is an aesthetic undertaking. Designing clothes for aesthetic effect is a creative undertaking. If a designer envisions her creations being worn on a certain shape of body, that's her prerogative. Even if we think her aesthetics are indecent or her politics are blinkered and decadent, we should respect her right to realize her creative goal. . . .

[The] main argument is that fashion shows should be regulated because they present an unhealthy ideal of beauty, to the public and therefore constitute a public health risk. I have no doubt this is true, but I don't want the government to suppress ideas just because the larger society considers those ideas to be destructive. . . .

Restricting the aesthetics of fashion shows is an infringement of First Amendment rights. Don't tell me that fashion show free speech is trivial. I won't argue too strenuously that fashion shows make an important contribution to public discourse, but censorship is censorship.

Lindsay Beyerstein,
"Emaciated Fashion Models and Occupational Health,"
Majikthise, *October 2, 2006.*

"the freedom of the designer" and "gazellelike" models. (Yeah, I laughed, too.) Pro-ban activists acknowledge that many designers and models will attempt to flout the new rules. But in that case, declared Carmen Gonzalez of Spain's Association in Defense of Attention for Anorexia and Bulimia, "the next step is to seek legislation, just like with tobacco."

Whoa, there, Carmen. I dislike catwalk freaks—pardon me, I mean human-gazelle hybrids—as much as the next normal woman. But surely most governments have better things to do than pass laws about what constitutes an acceptable butt size. Yes, without the coiffed tresses and acres of eyeliner, many models could be mistaken for those Third World kids that ex-celebs like Sally Struthers are always collecting money to feed. But that, ultimately, is their business. These women are paid to be models—not role models. The fashion world, no matter how unhealthy, is not Big Tobacco. (Though, come to think of it, Donatella Versace does bear a disturbing resemblance to Joe Camel.) And, with all due respect to the Madrid regional government, it is not the job of the industry to promote a healthy body image.

Indeed, there seems to be increasing confusion about what it is the "responsibility" of private industry to do. It is, for example, not the business of McDonald's to promote heart healthiness or slim waistlines. The company's central mission is, in fact, to sell enough fast, cheap, convenient eats to keep its stockholders rolling in dough. If this means loading up the food with salt and grease—because, as a chef friend once put it, "fat is flavor"—then that's what they're gonna do. Likewise, the fashion industry's goal has never been to make women feel good about themselves. (Stoking insecurity about consumers' stylishness—or lack thereof—is what the biz is all about.) Rather, the fashion industry's raison d'être is to sell glamour—to dazzle women with fantastical standards of beauty that, whether we're talking about a malnourished model or a $10,000 pair of gauchos, are, by design, far beyond the reach of regular people.

This is not to suggest that companies should be able to do whatever they like in the name of maximizing profits. False advertising, for instance, is a no-no. But long ago we decided that manufacturing and marketing products that could pose a significant risk to consumers' personal health and well-being—guns, booze, motorcycles, Ann Coulter—was okay so long as the dangers were fairly obvious (which is one reason Big Tobacco's secretly manipulating the nicotine levels in cigarettes to make them more addictive—not to mention lying about their health risks—was such bad form). The notion that the fashion industry should endure government meddling because its products or marketing techniques may pose an indirect risk to consumers by promoting an unhealthy desire for thinness seems dubious at best. More often than not, in the recognized trade-off between safety and freedom of choice, consumers tend to go with Option B.

Of course, whenever the issue of personal choice comes up, advocates of regulation typically point to the damage being done to impressionable young people. Be it consuming alcohol, overeating, smoking, watching violent movies, having anything other than straight, married, strictly procreation-aimed sex—whenever something is happening that certain people don't like, the first response is to decry the damage being done to our kids and start exploring legislative/regulatory remedies.

The Fashion Industry Should Be Left Alone

But here, again, the fashion industry's admittedly troubling affinity for women built like little boys doesn't seem to clear the hurdle for intervention. It was one thing for R.J. Reynolds to specifically target teens with its cigarette advertising. And, while I disagree with the attempts to make the war on fat the next war on smoking (for more on why, see here and here), you could at least make a similar argument that junk-food peddlers use kid-targeted advertising to sell youngsters everything from cupcakes to soda to french fries. But there's a difference between industries that specifically go after young consumers and those that happen to catch their eye—like, say, the fashion industry or Hollywood.

So let's give all those chain-smoking, Evian-guzzling, "gazelle-like" human-coatracks a break. In another couple of years, their metabolisms will slow down or they'll accidentally ingest some real food, and they'll be unceremoniously tossed off the catwalk like a bad pantsuit. Until then, in the name of personal choice, they should be allowed to strut their stuff—no matter how hideously skinny they are.

Periodical Bibliography

The following articles have been selected to supplement the diverse views presented in this chapter.

BBC News	"Crohn's 'Mistaken for Anorexia,'" March 20, 2005.
Martin Desseilles et al.	"Achalasia May Mimic Anorexia Nervosa, Compulsive Eating Disorder, and Obesity Problems," *Psychosomatics*, vol. 47, June 2006, pp. 270–71.
Amanda Easton	"I Became Bulimic After Watching MTV," *Teen People*, March 1, 2006, p. 105.
Economist	"Molecular Self-Loathing: Psychiatric Disorders and Immunity," October 1, 2005.
Jeff Evans	"Factors Driving Anorexia, Bulimia Are Complex," *Clinical Psychiatry News*, vol. 34, December 2006, pp. 49–50.
Carey Goldberg	"Binge Eating May Be Hereditary: Study Ties Genetics to Obesity Epidemic," *Boston Globe*, March 6, 2006.
P. Gorwood, A. Kipman, and C. Foulon	"The Human Genetics of Anorexia Nervosa," *European Journal of Pharmacology*, vol. 480, no. 1–3, November 7, 2003, pp. 163–70.
Natascha Kaminsky	"Skinny Model Ban Will Not Help," *MOSNews.com*, October 16, 2006. www.mosnews.com/feature/2006/10/06/skinnyban.shtml.
Margarita C.T. Slof-Op't Landt et al.	"Eating Disorders: From Twin Studies to Candidate Genes and Beyond," *Twin Research and Human Genetics*, vol. 8, no. 5, October 2005, pp. 467–82.
University of Pittsburgh Medical Center	"Specific Regions of Brain Implicated in Anorexia Nervosa, Finds Univ. of Pittsburgh Study," July 7, 2005.
Luisa Zargani et al.	"New Rules for Models," *Women's Wear Daily*, December 19, 2006.

OPPOSING VIEWPOINTS® SERIES

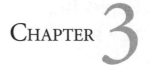

CHAPTER 3

What Role Does the Internet Play in Eating Disorders?

Chapter Preface

The entry page of the Web site is girlishly pretty. Against a muted peach background, images of a downcast young woman with garlands in her blonde hair and leaflike wings flank titles in ornate calligraphy. A disclaimer from the site creator describes this as a supportive, accepting site for people with anorexia and bulimia; tells visitors flatly that there is no information on this "pro-ana" site on how to develop these disorders; and orders them to exit if they're looking for instruction. According to the counter, 130,540 visitors have reached this disclaimer; nothing prevents them from clicking once more to anonymously enter and freely navigate the site.

Some of what they find there, well organized by topic, is unobjectionable and insightful: statistics ("The average U.S. woman is 5'4" and weighs 140 pounds. In contrast, the average U.S. model is 5'11" and weighs 117 pounds"), definitions ("The term *anorexia* literally means loss of appetite, but this is a misnomer. In fact, people with anorexia nervosa ignore hunger and thus control their desire to eat"), and medical information ("The acid in our intestines that digests our food comes up when a bulimic purges, slowly deteriorating the enamel that protects the teeth").

But the vast majority of the material presented on the site, no less insightful, is far more disturbing and unequivocally instructive. There are long lists of ideas to distract from hunger: "12. Wear a rubber band around your wrist and snap it when you want to eat. You'll train yourself not to think about eating." "106. Curl up in a ball if you have hunger pains."

There are page after page of "tips" for keeping an eating disorder secret: "Buy food. . . . If they see you come home with food, they just naturally assume that you eat it as well. Get things like crackers and cookies and dried fruits, keep them in your room, and carefully pack them out again later to throw away." "Check the fridge when nobody else is around. Find foods that you would have eaten and get rid of them; for example, three eggs and a piece of butter. Then if someone asks, you can say you had scrambled eggs and are really full." "Wear nail polish to hide the discoloring in your nails from lack of nutrients."

There are sample 200-calorie-per-day diets, lists of "safe" foods that supposedly burn more calories to metabolize than they contain, body-mass-index (BMI) calculators, and "tricks" for losing weight and throwing up as efficiently as possible: "43. Don't swallow—chew and spit." "63. Exercise 2 times the amount of calories you eat." "122. Carry a small container (like an eye dropper) filled with something inedible. When out with a group of ppl put a few drops on your food so you won't eat it." "Eat the healthy stuff first. . . . Since it's hard to get everything up, and since food comes up roughly in reverse order to how it went down, cushion the bad high-cal junk with safer foods."

This site has been active since 2004. Like hundreds of others, it has been shut down several times by Internet service providers in response to protest by eating disorder organizations, treatment facilities, and concerned families who argue that the pro-ana message promotes deadly illnesses and is too dangerous to allow. Like hundreds of others, it has reappeared on a different server, perhaps with a slightly different name or design, vowing to "go on stronger than ever." The viewpoints in this chapter examine the potential harm and value of pro-anorexia and pro-bulimia Web sites and the role of the Internet in general in the spread and treatment of eating disorders. Meanwhile, the still-active site urges visitors to come back soon; less than a day later, the entry-page counter has jumped by more than a thousand.

| *"Pro-ana sites are the antithesis of self-help websites for recovering anorexics."*

Pro-Ana Web Sites Are Dangerous and Should Be Condemned

Elanor Taylor

The controversial pro-ana (pro–anorexia nervosa) or pro-mia (pro-bulimia) movement emerged as an online subculture in 2001 when several Web sites glorifying eating disorders were featured in major news magazines and television shows. Since then, efforts by Web hosts to shut down such sites have had limited results. In the following viewpoint, Elanor Taylor describes pro-ana sites' harmful influences and contradictory messages, and questions the ethics and morality of allowing the sites to exist. Elanor Taylor is a consultant researcher and writer for the Social Issues Research Center, a British independent nonprofit organization that monitors, assesses, and debates global sociocultural trends.

As you read, consider the following questions:

1. Whom do pro-ana and pro-mia Web sites target, according to Taylor?

Elanor Taylor, "Totally in Control," Social Issues Research Center (SIRC), July 11, 2002. www.sirc.org/articles/totally_in_control2.shtml. Reproduced by permission of the author.

2. According to the author, what material presented on pro-ana sites triggers or reinforces dangerously unhealthy eating habits?

3. What flaws does Taylor find in the pro-ana message that anorexia is a display of strength, not illness?

Type anorexia or bulimia into an Internet search engine and the results will typically consist of help, information and support for people who are suffering from or know someone who is suffering from an eating disorder. Type in "pro-anorexia," or "pro-ana/pro-mia," and a very different picture emerges. With titles like Starving For Perfection, Anorexic Nation, 2b-Thin and Totally in Control, pro-ana sites are the antithesis of self-help websites for recovering anorexics. So much so that every site has a disclaimer on the front page:

> This site does not encourage that you develop an eating disorder. This is a site for those who ALREADY have an eating disorder and do not wish to go into recovery.... If you do not already have an eating disorder, better it is that you do not develop one now. You may wish to leave. (ana-by-choice.com)

> **DiScLaImEr: This iS a PrO-eD SiTe... iF yOu Do NoT hAvE aN eAtinG disOrDeR oR aRe YoU aRe In ReCoVeRy YoU sHoUlD NoT view this site.... i Am NoT ReSpOn-SiBLe FoR yOuR aCtioNs.. LeAvE iF you CaNt HaNdLe iT*** (2b Thin)

Pro-ana sites are emphatically not for those who are in recovery, regard themselves as victims, or even regard themselves as ill. They are targeted at those who *"believe that the Ana way is the only way to live,"* who feel that anorexia is the right lifestyle choice for them, and will allow them to achieve happiness and perfection.

A Disturbed View of Anorexia

Statistically, eating disorders are most common in young women; sufferers are often portrayed as hapless victims of a ruthless consumer culture. *Victim* is the key word here; it is generally thought that nobody *wants* to be anorexic, that anorexia is a disease, and that sufferers *want* to get better. Pro-ana sites turn these preconceptions on their heads. One site goes so far as to distinguish "anorexics" from "rexies," the idea being that if you identify yourself as an "anorexic" then the site is not for you:

> You may already know the difference between us rexies and anorexics! If u want sympathy for your "disease", you are anorexic. If you want respect and admiration for your lifestyle of choice, you are a rexic... Anorexics die. Rexies don't. Have we understood the difference? This site is for us rexies, who are proud of our accomplishments, and the accomplishments that lie ahead. we will never die. (Rexia-World)

The emphasis is moved from self-destruction to self-control; in the words of one "rexie," "*A good ana doesn't die.*" If you are using anorexia as a means of self-destruction then, according to these girls, you simply aren't doing it right. Key ideas are strength, will, achievement, fulfilment; eating disorders are portrayed as a means of achieving perfection and of forming an elite, a group of humans who have successfully "mastered" or "governed" their bodies.

Unsurprisingly, these claims to strength, independence and health fail to ring true when a small but significant minority of sites are left unattended because their controller is "having to take it easy for a bit" or "has gone into recovery." In one case, an online journal, message board and support group was being maintained from a hospital bed. In light of this, the protestation "*we will never die*" sounds more like a cry of rebellion than a promise.

Contradictory Messages

While a number of sites claim to subscribe to the view that good anorexics "don't go too far," some contain material that would suggest the opposite. Almost all have a "thinspiration" picture gallery, displaying photographs of stick-thin models and ana beauty ideals. Most feature Kate Moss at her thinnest and a decidedly emaciated Jodie Kidd as examples of "perfection." A significant minority go further, providing pictures of women in the last stages of anorexia, hollow-cheeked and utterly fleshless. Pro-ana artwork is similarly varied. One picture in particular, which appears on a number of sites, features a fairy-like, unearthly creature amid a mass of psychedelic blue swirls. The caption reads:

> Infinity is so damn sweet / Your mortal earth cannot compete / Starving for the other shore / I will not eat! / Say it loud & say it now / I'm anorexic & I'm proud. (ana's underground grotto)

This kind of material renders the noisy preaching of the gospel of "empowerment" by the rexie-sisterhood crew a distasteful joke. Pro-ana websites are a mass of contradictions; with every supportive post on a bulletin board about the dangers of excessive purging ("try washing your mouth out with bicarbonate of soda afterwards, it'll protect your teeth from the acid in your puke"), there is another entitled "Please somebody help me," "I really need to die" or "My parents are forcing me to go to hospital and I'm scared I'll get fat."

Despite extensive media coverage, an air of mystery still hangs around pro-ana/pro-mia websites. This is perhaps because the most basic questions about their existence are often ignored in favour of more sensational material. The following questions and answers are an attempt to make sense of the wealth of contradictory material that is the web-based pro-ana/pro-mia movement.

What Does Pro-Ana/Pro-Mia Mean?

Pro-ana stands for pro-anorexia. Pro-mia stands for pro-bulimia. "Pro" does *not* mean, "supports the promotion of."

Accomplices to Suicide

Many experts find . . . pro–eating-disorder sites appalling. "It's one of the few times in history that someone has come out and said that a very dangerous illness is a good idea, and here's how to do it," says Christopher Athas, vice president of the National Association of Anorexia Nervosa and Associated Disorders. "They talk about First Amendment rights. But this is like shouting fire. . . . These people with these sites claim that they are representing a lifestyle, but they are representing a dangerous illness." Researchers have demonstrated that eating disorders can lead to anxiety, depression, alcoholism, substance abuse, self-mutilation and suicide.

But the pro-ana and pro-mia sites . . . tend to gloss over that kind of information—and the fact that people with anorexia are more than 56 times more likely than their peers to commit suicide, says Cynthia Bulik, director of the eating-disorders program at the University of North Carolina at Chapel Hill. "People who are posting to these sites are accomplices to suicide." . . .

In November [2006] the Academy for Eating Disorders issued a warning about the proliferation of sites promoting anorexia and asked government officials and Internet service providers to require warning screens for them. AED president Eric van Furth suggested a statement like "Warning: anorexia nervosa is a potentially deadly illness. The site you are about to enter provides material that may be detrimental to your health."

Karen Springen, "Study Looks at Pro-Anorexia Web Sites,"
Newsweek, *December 10, 2006, MSNBC.com.*
www.msnbc.msn.com/id/16098915/site/newsweek.

Most disclaimers contain something along the lines of "If you do not have an eating disorder then it is better for you if you do not develop one," although the more hard-line sites often use challenging language, such as "If you can't handle it, leave."

Pro-ana sites are for those who are *already* anorexics, who *want* to be "triggered" and are looking for advice, tips and support from fellow anorexics to help them become "better" anorexics. "Pro-ana" symbolises the choice *not* to go into recovery; if you are pro-ana then by definition you have chosen to live wholeheartedly as an anorexic, at least for the time being.

What Is New About the Message Projected by Pro-Ana Sites?

The emphasis on superiority, empowerment and pride through self-control. As one site puts it, in response to a number of complaints about its pro-ana content and picture gallery: "The difference is that you lot moan about your fat thighs and then sit on the couch eating cookies. We moan about our fat thighs and then go out for a lovely long run."

The use of political language. Many talk of anorexics as "the elite," and present the anorexic lifestyle as a rejection of conventional "weak" values. . . . Most pro-ana sites claim to be concerned with self-control and achievement, although some material suggests that this should be taken with a pinch of salt.

Pro-anas claim that most people want to be thinner, and that they are just making that wish a reality for themselves, rather than engaging in a form of self-harm. Ultimately, anorexia will always be self-destructive; whether it is recognised as such by the sufferer is another question.

Most of those who visit pro-ana sites do not want to go into recovery. There are few other places where an anorexic could be honest about this without causing distress.

Pro-ana sites encourage pride and a sense of belonging to a community; some [visitors] want to be "better anorexics," to get thinner with the help of tips and support from fellow anorexics. Some feel persecuted and misunderstood everywhere else for not wanting to go into recovery. The websites also have a certain underground cachet. They allow the anorexic to feel like a pro-active rebel rather than a walking disorder.

Are Pro-Ana Sites Being Censored?

Some servers, e.g., Yahoo, have simply stopped allowing certain sites to function in response to complaints and extensive media coverage on the issue of pro-ana. While this has prevented further complaints about the servers, it has proved ineffective in its primary goal of getting rid of pro-ana material on the web. Some sites now claim to be "diet sites" rather than pro-ana, yet contain the same material, tips and so on.

Pro ana sites pose a problem for non-anorexics. They especially pose a problem for those who care for someone with an eating disorder. This is because they allow people with eating disorders to get together and support each other in their struggle to achieve their goals, not towards recovery but towards thinness, "perfection," and "the perfect body." Knowledge of their existence entails a dilemma—is it ethically acceptable to allow sites which encourage unrealistic aspiration towards self-destructive goals to continue to function? We may as well censor the pages of the major fashion glossies, with their features on "How star x slimmed to x stone [pounds] one month after the birth of her first child," or "The latest diets to help you fight the flab." Fashion magazines will often provide advice on exercise and "healthy" eating alongside pictures of genuinely underweight models, many of who appear on the "thinspiration" sections of pro-ana websites. To censor pro-ana sites in the face of this kind of material seems hypocritical, to say the least. Yet the feeling that there is something "not quite right," maybe even immoral, about their continued existence persists.

Contrary to popular misconception, volitional anorexics possess the most iron-cored, indomitable wills of all. Our way is not that of the weak.

If we ever completely tapped that potential in our midst, and applied it to other areas outside eating habits and body sculpting, the fact is, we could change the world.

Completely.

Maybe even rule it.

Is THAT what they are so afraid of?. . . Could it simply be that those who wield their pathetic little naked-emperor reign so irresponsibly and selfishly do NOT want word getting out to "the masses" of how simple a matter it is to throw off their chains and exist self-directed? (ana's underground grotto)

This voice is articulate, strong, and most of all rebellious. In borrowed political rhetoric, the anorexic's impulse to control is inflated into a quality that could change the world. It is fair to argue that the anorexic capacity for will power and self-control is truly remarkable. If harnessed for different purposes, that capacity could arguably produce some impressive results. However, it is unlikely that any anorexic, before recovery, would be capable of devoting the same level of time and attention to any area other than their own weight control.

The anorexic's dedication and perfectionism is born of obsession, which is in itself a product of various highly complex factors, internal and external. To interpret anorexia as a demonstration of nothing more than admirable self-control is to subscribe to the myth perpetuated by the pro-ana movement that anorexia is a display of strength, rather than illness. . . .

Anorexia is not a lifestyle choice. It is an illness. The pro-ana claims to political minority status are disturbing and delusional. That is not to suggest that anorexics, even pro-anorexics, should be deprived of a platform on which to communicate. Censorship of pro-ana sites is inappropriate and ineffective, especially when the infinitely more disturbing material that can be found on the web—pro-handgun lobbies, cam girl sites, fascist propaganda—is considered. What is worrying is not the existence of pro-ana sites, but the way that these sites present eating disorders as an alternative lifestyle choice, and encourage both those who suffer and those who don't to subscribe to that myth. The softer sites use the language of "girl-power," the more militant sites use the language of Marx. Both display the horrific irony of women rendering themselves weaker in the name of strength.

> *"Pro-ana blogs and websites are ... a valuable source of information about the lives and psychological make-up of those who have the disorder."*

Pro-Ana Web Sites Are Valuable and Have a Right to Exist

Angie Rankman

In the following viewpoint, Angie Rankman argues that the misguided claims and dangerous rationales of pro-ana Web sites can be understood, exposed, and opposed much more effectively if the sites are allowed to operate openly. Because anorexia is potentially lethal and notoriously difficult to treat, she maintains, medical professionals should take advantage of the insights pro-ana sites offer. Censorship only strengthens the resolve of pro-ana sites and drives them underground, Rankman says, where they will continue to promote a skewed, unscrutinized vision of eating disorders. Angie Rankman writes on women's issues and is a contributor to Aphrodite Women's Health, *an independent, Web-based news publication and discussion forum.*

As you read, consider the following questions:

1. How do pro-ana Web sites portray anorexia as a lifestyle choice, not a disorder, according to Rankman?

2. According to the author, how can allowing pro-ana sites to operate freely benefit medical professionals and the anorexic's friends and family?

3. In Rankman's view, what are the two most harmful effects of censoring pro-ana Web sites?

It has been argued that the Internet is a democratic, equalizing force within society, and the plethora of views and opinions on personal websites perhaps reinforces that idea. But with the proliferation of porn and file sharing sites, democracy and free speech have had their limits tested. And pushing the envelope with the best (and worst) of them is the pro-anorexic social movement called "pro-ana." A rapid decline in the visibility of pro-ana sites on the Internet may be vindication enough for those in favor of censoring pro-ana sites, but a question mark hangs over the censorship of the online pro-ana movement. Yes, the sites might well be away from view, but is it a case of out-of-sight out-of-mind?

A Valuable Window for Families and Treatment Providers

Pro-ana is a social movement among girls (mostly) who use websites, forums and blogs to advocate the idea that anorexia is a *lifestyle* choice rather than a disorder. The pro-ana sites are filled with forums and discussion boards targeting girls who share the same philosophy. Pro-ana sites portray thin celebrities (dubbed "thinspirations") such as Paris Hilton, Angelina Jolie and Kate Moss as role models; and links to other sites such as *Skinny Secrets, Fasting Girls, Hunger Hurts but Starving Works* and *Dying to Be Thin* help to normalize anorexia in readers' minds. One site explains that their "website is to help those who are wanting to become anorexic, and for those who are feeling weak," where weak means eating.

Censorship Will Drive
Pro-Ana Sites Underground

[Karin] Davis is the program coordinator for the National Eating Disorder Information Centre. While Davis says pro-ana sites can perpetuate eating disorders, she doesn't necessarily agree with the movement to ban them. "I think everyone is very quick to assume that pulling the sites off the servers is the best response, and I question it," says Davis. "For one thing, we're up against free speech. Plus, by shutting them down they're going to be pushed further underground." According to Davis, more research needs to be done. With supporters already on the defensive, banning the sites could alienate members of the pro-ana community from professionals who can help.

She also stresses the importance of not demonizing pro-ana supporters. "The people creating these are not evil," she says. "They obviously find some sort of support and comfort from connecting to others who are struggling with the same thing."

Sarah Vermunt, "Boxing Ana," Shift.com, 2003.
www.healthyplace.com/communities/Eating_Disorders/Site
/story_pro_ana.htm.

Pro-ana sites often try to support their arguments by posting articles like "UW Study: Eat Less, Live Longer!" and "Fewer calories = Longer Life!," which support eating less, but are taken out of context and extrapolated to the extreme. But the real power of these sites comes from the reinforcing and normalizing of the belief among members that anorexia sufferers have merely chosen to live a certain way, much as someone would choose a style of clothing. Usually pro-ana sites don't actively recruit members, although you could say that they definitely encourage it, and many members already have a history of anorexia. Pro-ana sites were at their height during the period 2000–2003, but since then there has been a dramatic drop off rate, put down to heavy Internet censorship of the sites.

Having the pro-ana (there are also offshoots like pro-bella and pro-mia for bulimia) philosophy explained to you is both surprising and shocking, and one's first reaction is to side with those who want to ban outright all online traces of the movement. After some contemplation, however, you remind yourself that these girls are the sufferers of a very dangerous and misunderstood disorder, and that the pro-ana sites are likely just another manifestation of anorexia. Sure, you could treat this symptom—as I'm sure advocates of censorship believe they are doing—but ignores the fact that the pro-ana blogs and websites are also a valuable source of information about the lives and psychological make-up of those who have the disorder.

Treatment and prevention of anorexia has always been a daunting task for health professionals. Some health workers explain that it is easier to get young females off hard drugs than it is for them to treat anorexia, and a recent Penn State University study claimed that: "The mortality rate associated with anorexia is 12 times higher than the death rate of other causes of death for females 15–24 years old."

The fact that anorexia is such an unforgiving and dangerous disorder is why pro-ana sites are so important, as they can act as a window into what may have started the disorder in the first place, and what it is that keeps the disorder ticking along. And even if you don't consider that there is any medical merit in keeping these sites open, wouldn't it be better to know what young anorexics are thinking and feeling than not? Critics of this approach may argue that this is a mercenary way of getting to grips with a dangerous syndrome like anorexia, and that the censorship of such sites is the only option available. But censorship on the Internet is a tricky business and pro-ana sites are still easily found.

Censorship Only Drives Anorexia Sites Underground

In fact, the pro-ana sites, and their self-harm counterparts, have merely slipped out of mainstream view and gone underground; a scenario that has for a long time been associated with censorship. Hosts of pro-ana sites have become experts at hiding the intentions behind their site, often posting disclaimers on their entry pages that their site is for the support of people with anorexia. Well, I guess they're not lying, as they do support individuals who are anorexic, it's just that the support offered is how anorexics can *maintain* the disorder. Lifestyle, remember? One site has a whole page devoted to telling other pro-ana advocates: "How to stop getting your ana site deleted." Tips include not listing your site with high profile search engines like Google, saving work in case of deletion, and: "Always put up a disclaimer note on your main page telling visitors why it was created. This is so they don't think your [sic] making the page to *ahem* 'turn teenage girls into anorexics.'" Stealth like this is alarming, and more worryingly, it makes it very difficult to sort the harmful websites from those offering genuine support.

The ability to communicate globally is one of the most powerful tools that humans have at their disposal. The Internet is a facilitator of this ability and can therefore aid in fostering community care and responsibility through complex social networks. However, it seems evident that we are still at a critical juncture of our online evolution, as there is still much about our own humanity that shocks, frightens and offends sensibilities.

When anorexic young females began writing about their lives in blogs and forums a whole new line of communication instantly opened up, and with that came new hope for parents, health professionals and close friends who have been trying to understand the disorder and the young women for years. But instead of embracing this open dialogue, society displayed moral outrage and sought fit to respond by shutting down the sites, and along with it an invaluable source of insight into a vexing and deadly disorder. Worse still, censorship has led to pro-ana sites employing new tactics to avoid detection and deletion; often, of all things, portraying themselves as anorexia *help* sites; an arguably much more dangerous framing.

It's deeply regrettable that censorship has achieved nothing more than burying the problem away from mainstream view. Hidden away, pro-ana sites continue to flourish away from the prying eyes of those who can and wish to help. Shame on us, if out-of-sight out-of-mind is the best that we can do for those suffering this insidious disorder.

> *"Pro-eating disorder Web sites . . . ratio-nalize and affirm the very behavior that defines the disease. They also pack-age their message in alluring colors, music and designs that attract young girls."*

Controversial Web Sites Glorify Anorexia and Bulimia

Kristen Depowski and Kelly Hart

In the following viewpoint, Kristen Depowski and Kelly Hart contend that impressionable young women, already culturally predisposed to idealize thinness and to dislike their bodies, are dangerously vulnerable to hundreds of easily accessible Web sites that glamorize eating disorders and give explicit instructions in how to be a "better" anorexic. The only genuine support this community offers, the authors warn, is misguided mourning for its followers when they die of their disorders. Kristen Depowski and Kelly Hart report for the ABC News Law and Justice Unit, correspondents, attorneys, and interns who research and produce legal stories for the network's news shows.

Kristen Depowski and Kelly Hart, "'Pro-Ana' Web Sites Glorify Eating Disorders," ABC News online, June 13, 2006. http://abcnews.go.com/Health/print?id=2068728.

As you read, consider the following questions:

1. How many pro-eating disorder Web sites exist and how frequently are they visited, in the authors' estimate?

2. In what ways does the glorification of eating disorders approach religious intensity, according to Depowski and Hart?

3. What age group is particularly vulnerable to the glamorization of anorexia, according to ANAD spokesperson Annie Hayashi?

Bathing suit season is upon us, and more people are hitting the gym and starting new diets trying to shed unwanted pounds.

But for millions of Internet-savvy teens, a dangerous alternative is just a click away—countless Web sites that glorify, promote and teach that eating disorders aren't a disease, but a "lifestyle choice." This, despite the fact that eating disorders are one of the most deadly mental illnesses in the country.

Annie Hayashi, spokesperson for the National Association of Anorexia Nervosa and Associated Disorders (ANAD), says that 6 percent of people with eating disorders will eventually die from the disease. "We believe that the pro-eating disorder sites are not only destructive but dangerous," said Hayashi. "They give legitimacy to people who can't recover and are triggering for people who are trying to recover."

There are about 500 Web sites that offer tips on how to become anorexic or bulimic. The popularity of what are known as "pro-ana" (pro-anorexia) and "pro-mia" (pro-bulimia) Web sites has increased in recent years. They attract mostly teenage girls and young women, often getting thousands of hits a day.

Most Web sites are run by self-proclaimed "rexies"—individuals who celebrate their eating disorders. Some even call it a religion, reciting psalms and offering prayers to their goddess "Ana." Many of the sites feature "thinspirational" photos, which depict the skin-and-bones of emaciated models and celebrities.

On one site, www.ceruleanbutterfly.com, the philosophy is frighteningly blunt: "One day I will be thin enough. Just the bones, no disfiguring flesh. Just the pure clean shape of me, bones. That is what we all are, what we're made up of and everything else is just storage, deposit, waste."

Most of the Web sites give tips on the most effective way to starve oneself. One site recommends "taking antacids" to "help reduce hunger pains" and constantly drinking coffee, diet soda and chewing gum so "you won't feel hungry." Other tips from similar sites—get manicures to hide your split and broken nails, shower in cold water to burn calories, and wear multiple layers of clothing to hide your weight loss.

Trying to Shut Down Sites

Experts say these so-called pro-ED (pro-eating disorder) Web sites are potentially deadly, particularly because they rationalize and affirm the very behavior that defines the disease. They also package their message in alluring colors, music and designs that attract young girls.

According to Hayashi, "11-, 12-, and 13-year-old girls see and visit these sites and emulate the behavior." She points out that pre-adolescence is a challenging and confusing time, and teenagers can easily fall prey to the obsessions of this self-destructive and tightly-knit community, resulting in sometimes tragic consequences.

"They have an emotional predisposition . . . and are already feeling isolated, with low self-esteem," Hayashi said.

In order to shut down the dangerous Internet forums, Hayashi says ANAD spends a lot of time searching the Internet, identifying pro-eating disorder sites, then contacting and informing the web servers. Hayashi explains that the only way

The Allure of Pro-Ana Web Sites Is Stronger than Ever

Anorexia—a disease that affects one to two percent of females in the United States—isn't the hidden behavior it used to be. The Internet has connected thousands of anorexics and has enabled them to share every detail of their ana (a nickname for the disorder) experience with anyone who will read it. Once among the fastest-growing topics on the web, pro-ana websites have decreased in numbers since 2001, when large domains like Yahoo! began shutting many of them down. But sites like MySpace.com, faccbook.com and LiveJournal.com have helped bring the networks back, allowing women to announce their latest calorie cut or celebrate another pound lost. And the threat has evolved. Through daily communication via post, note and message, the newer sites offer participants personal, round-the-clock cheerleading throughout the process of depriving their bodies.

There are more than 100 communities on LiveJournal and about 10 MySpace groups that list pro-anorexia as an interest. Facebook groups including "S4P ... I need perfection" and "**Pro-Ana**" promote anorexia, sharing slogans like "Hunger is only a feeling" and "NOTHING tastes as good as being THIN feels."

Kristi Eaton, "Health: The Skinny on Pro-Ana," MSNBC.com, November 15, 2006.

to get these dangerous sites off the Web is to notify the web servers, which can shut them down for violating the terms and conditions of their Internet agreement.

Another strategy ANAD uses is to report that the various sites contain pornographic images of half-clothed and emaciated young girls, many of whom are underage. While servers such as Yahoo, Lycos and MySpace have been particularly responsive to removing pro-ana and pro-mia Web sites, according to Hayashi, some sites have refused to cooperate with ANAD's requests, citing First Amendment arguments.

Advocacy sites like ANAD offer tips for parents to recognize the early-warning signs of eating disorders. Among them: a sudden interest in calorie counting, wearing baggy clothing, excessive caffeine consumption, fanatical exercise and a general obsession with weight. These groups urge parents to monitor their children's Internet activity, and keep a watchful eye out for pro-ana and pro-mia sites.

As Hayashi says, parents' vigilance could be a matter of life and death. "The danger of these sites is the sense of community and support they provide. A community some know will mourn them when, not if, they die."

> *"The technologies of the Internet offer a very useful tool for mental health care providers to reach a wider range of girls suffering from or at risk for eating disorders."*

The Internet Is an Important Tool in Recovery from Eating Disorders

Theresia Laksmana

Although eating disorder information and counsel found on the Internet must be carefully assessed for accuracy and reliability, Theresia Laksmana concludes in the following viewpoint, the Internet is a great resource for both sufferers and treatment professionals. Key benefits include anonymity, round-the-clock access, and potentially frequent contact with therapists at low cost. Theresia Laksmana is a 2003 graduate of the University of Pennsylvania and a contributor to the university's annual undergraduate research journal Perspectives in Psychology.

As you read, consider the following questions:

1. What are the advantages of online eating disorder support groups, according to Laksmana?

Theresia Laksmana, "Eating Disorders and the Internet: The Therapeutic Possibilities," University of Pennsylvania, *Perspectives in Psychology*, vol. 5, Spring 2002, pp. 35–41. Reproduced by permission of the author.

2. In the author's view, how can the Internet serve as a therapeutic tool by physicians who treat eating-disorder patients?

3. How can Internet-delivered programs such as Student Bodies actually prevent eating disorders, according to Laksmana?

Over the past few decades, the increasing amount of eating disorders has become a topic of concern. Many attribute this "phenomenon" to societal factors, such as the standards of beauty set by the media, fashion and entertainment industries. However, most people today are misinformed about eating disorders and underestimate the life-threatening dangers involved. Many people do not realize that the mortality rate of anorexia nervosa has been found to be between 5–20%. Funding for health care services, especially eating disorder programs, has decreased over the past few years. Thus, it has become even more important to develop efficient and cost-effective ways to inform, treat, and prevent eating disorders. The emergence of the Internet has become a hopeful medium for the implementation of these programs.

Eating Disorder Websites

The advent of the Internet has given individuals the ability to access all kinds of information from the comfort and privacy of their homes and offices. Not only does the Internet supply a limitless range of information, but it also introduces us to millions of other users from around the globe, allowing us to talk to anyone, anywhere, at any time. Clearly, with the Internet's fast-paced growth, it was only a matter of time before the mental health world would begin taking advantage of its resources. Amidst the wealth of information the Internet offers, thousands of websites have been devoted to the issue of eating disorders.

It has been difficult to make people fully aware of the dangers of eating disorders because of society's misconcep-

Internet Resources Are Confidential, Convenient, Affordable, and Effective

Younger eating disordered individuals in particular may first seek help and advice online, out of fears of admitting such a problem to parents or loved ones—after all, it is much easier to write about bingeing and purging than it is to look Mom in the eye and admit such a secret.... For those living in rural areas, or, as is common in the United States, lacking insurance to pay for formal therapy, online support may become crucial.

Those individuals already participating in therapy, be it one-on-one or group treatment, may also find internet connections useful between sessions. While episodes of eating disordered behaviour should always be thoroughly discussed in therapy, it is sometimes a tremendous help to log on at 2am on a Saturday night when the urge to over-exercise strikes.

Tiffany Hiles, "Recovery Resources Online," Sheena's Place,
fall 2006. www.sheenasplace.org.

tions and ignorance about them. Although the Internet can educate individuals about eating disorders, vast amounts of false information on this subject also exist, as is the case with most everything else on the internet....

Nevertheless, although ensuring the accuracy of information on the Internet is a recurring problem, individuals can find comfort in knowing that information provided by government mental health websites and sites run by eating disorder organizations is most often reliable.

Along with many of the misconceptions about eating disorders, a great deal of stigmatism also exists regarding eating disorders. Having illnesses that are perceived as embarrassing or socially disgracing, such as eating disorders often are, lead people to seek support of others who share their condition. Thus, it is no wonder that eating disorder support groups have evolved over the Internet. Online support groups can be accessed through all sorts of services such as AOL and USENET. In chat rooms people can come together to talk and share stories about their common disorder. They often find support from those who can sympathize with their experiences, and they can pass on information about the best treatments and how they and their families can best cope with it. Today, several eating disorder newsgroups and chat rooms exist for individuals to share their personal experiences and learn information on how best to deal with the disorder.

Advantages of Online Eating Disorder Support Groups

The Internet is accessible at any time of the day, all year round. Messages can be posted and e-mails can be sent at any time, by anyone in the world, from the privacy of one's own home. It is relatively cost efficient and easy to use. There is no set time that people must write e-mails or enter chat rooms, and individuals do not have to work their schedule around online group sessions as they do for face-to-face sessions. In one study on an eating disorder newsgroup, A.J. Winzelberg found that two thirds of the messages were posted between 6pm and 7am, a time when support from healthcare professionals or face-to-face support groups would have been least accessible.

Many hospitals and community clinics offer support groups, yet many individuals turn to Internet support groups. Internet support groups offer anonymity; and in cases like eating disorders, being able to seek support for a disease while still being able to remain anonymous is highly desirable. For some, remaining anonymous is a way of reaching out for help while not having to admit to those close to them that they have a problem. Girls can share their similar experiences and can often help one another, regardless of whom they are talking to.

Anonymity also allows for elimination of socio-demographic factors like age, race, and socioeconomic status. As a result, differences in social status, which are normally more visible in face-to-face sessions, can be minimized, and issues of physical attractiveness and social skills are neutralized. Anonymity reduces the shame and embarrassment that people sometimes associate with their eating disorders. . . .

Internet-based Eating Disorder Therapies

The difficulty in treating eating disorders and the amount of relapse has led physicians to start using e-mail as an adjunct to therapy. Its uses can range from the simple task of scheduling appointments to more in depth correspondence in which weekly e-mail reports are required of the patient.

A case study done by J. Yager (2000) illustrates the correspondence between him and four of his patients. After each treatment, patients submitted evaluations of the mandatory use of e-mail to supplement treatment. All the patients found it helpful, most importantly because it met a "demand feeding" schedule, meaning they were able to write whenever they felt the need to "speak" to the doctor. They could write the mandatory e-mails as their schedules permitted, and having to do them almost daily kept them in constant awareness of their behaviors. The constant contact via e-mails increased the frequency and amount of time with their clinician, forging a stronger relationship with the doctor and making it more comfortable for them to say whatever they wanted either in the e-mails or in the therapy sessions. . . .

For some girls, there are advantages to using e-mail as the only means of communication. Using e-mail eliminates much of the status disparity between therapist and patient. Along with this, some patients may feel more comfortable with their therapist and may interact less formally than they otherwise might feel comfortable doing in an office, face-to-face. For some, avoidance of face-to-face confrontation makes it easier for them to be honest about their discussions. Knowing that the physician will not be focusing on their physical appearances is comforting and allows them to feel less pressured. In this experiment, anonymity was maintained, to a great extent. This is very important for sufferers since many do not seek treatment because of shame and guilt. However, it should be noted that in this study, physicians were given their college e-mail addresses so that, in case of an emergency, they would be able to obtain proper medical care for the patient. . . .

Prevention Programs

Less than 1% of the young adult female population suffers from anorexia while about 1–2% of the population suffers from bulimia nervosa. More than 10% of college women are thought to have sub-clinical bulimia nervosa, and 25% of college women are thought to be at risk for developing eating disorders. For this reason, it is clear why finding an effective prevention program is imperative. Unfortunately, prevention programs for eating disorders have not had very satisfactory outcomes. Their effectiveness has been questioned, with some studies showing that it can in fact be more harmful than beneficial for individuals. Furthermore, funding for prevention programs has been scarce because, even as eating disorders is a widespread mental health problem, its prevalence is not comparable to such disorders as depression or drug abuse.

One Internet-based prevention program, however, has been shown to be effective and cost-efficient. Participants in an Internet-delivered computer assisted health education program (CAHE) called Student Bodies have exhibited significant decreases in body image dissatisfaction. The Student Bodies program, modeled from self-help treatments for eating disorders, incorporates a moderator-mediated electronic newsgroup used as a forum by participants to discuss readings and assignments. It was designed to decrease body image dissatisfaction, a probable risk factor for the development of eating disorders. Developed by eating disorder researchers at Stanford University, the program was first run as four separate trials between 1995 through 1998. Each successive trial, using a modified version of the program, showed improved results in the reduction of body image concerns and eating disorder psychopathology. . . .

It is obvious that the technologies of the Internet offer a very useful tool for mental health care providers to reach a wider range of girls suffering from or at risk for eating disorders. Perhaps the most important development is the success of the Student Bodies prevention program. Determining the factors that are most effective in the program will allow physicians to better understand the pathology of the disorder and perhaps aid them in modifying the current treatments. Hopefully, if this program can be safely provided to girls all around the country, the epidemic of eating disorders might come to a halt, or at the very least, exhibit a decrease in the number of incidences.

Periodical Bibliography

The following articles have been selected to supplement the diverse views presented in this chapter.

Academy of Eating Disorders	"AED Position Statement on Pro-Anorexia Web Sites." www.aedweb.org/policy/pro-anorexia _sites.cfm.
Mark L. Norris et al.	"Ana and the Internet: A Review of Pro-Anorexia Websites," *International Journal of Eating Disorders*, vol. 39, no. 6, September 2006, pp. 443–47.
Thomas Papworth	"Shut It, Ana! (You're Only Free If You're Not Wrong)," *Liberal Polemic*, January 6, 2007. http://liberalpolemic.blogspot.com/2007/01/ shut-it-ana-youre-only-free-if-youre.html.
PC Magazine	"Study: Anorexics, Bulimics Learn Methods Online," December 5, 2006. www.pcmag.com.
Page Rockwell	"Student Bodies, Student Selves," *Salon*, November 1, 2006. www.salon.com/mwt/ broadsheet/2006/11/01/eating_disorders/ index.html.
Karen Springen	"Mixed Messages," *Newsweek*, December 10, 2006, MSNBC.com. www.msnbc.msn.com/id/ 16098915/site/newsweek/.
C. Barr Taylor et al.	"Prevention of Eating Disorders in At-Risk College-Age Women," *Archives of General Psychiatry*, vol. 63, August 2006, pp. 881–88.
Jenny L. Wilson et al.	"Surfing for Thinness: A Pilot Study of Pro-Eating Disorder Web Site Usage in Adolescents with Eating Disorders," *Pediatrics*, vol. 118, December 2006, pp. 1635–43.

OPPOSING
VIEWPOINTS®
SERIES

CHAPTER 4

How Should Eating Disorders Be Treated?

Chapter Preface

Eating disorder (ED) experts often cite the following statistics about anorexia nervosa: Approximately 50 percent of sufferers fully recover from their disorder. Thirty percent can be expected to partially recover with recurring treatment as needed. The remaining 20 percent of anorexia cases resist all treatment and must be considered chronic; a high percentage of these sufferers will eventually die of complications associated with the disorder, including suicide.

According to the ED advocacy organization Anna Westin Foundation, these statistics could be significantly improved if entrenched barriers to insurance coverage for eating disorders are removed. Founders Kitty and Mark Westin's twenty-one-year-old daughter, Anna, took her own life in 2001 after a five-year struggle with anorexia. Their experience convinced them that anorexia requires earlier, more intensive, and longer post-hospitalization treatment than most health insurance policies allow, which means most anorexia patients are released too soon from (and cannot afford to continue) life-saving treatment programs, and relapse. The foundation argues that state governments and managed care "must be forced to provide the necessary treatments," including:

- Mental Health Parity laws that forbid insurance companies to impose lower day and visit limits, higher co-pays and deductibles, and lower annual and lifetime spending caps for mental disorders;

- hospitalization based on abnormal vital signs (e.g., blood pressure, heart rate, body temperature) and laboratory tests, not on the *DSM-IV* requirement that weight must fall below 85 percent of normal;

- hospital discharge based on the patient's psychosocial improvement, never solely on weight gain;

- partial hospitalization at a level of five days a week, eight hours a day, switching to reduced outpatient care only if weight, blood and urine, and vital signs are carefully monitored.

- insurers that deny requests for care or base approval on other-than-accepted guidelines must accept full responsibility for the patient's life.

Health insurance companies defend existing standards of coverage for eating disorders by arguing that eating disorders are psychiatric, not biological, illnesses and that therefore, as with other mental disorders, more than a month or two of hospitalization per year cannot be justified, and by pointing to data that indicate that no treatment is effective against severe, chronic anorexia, and thus, likewise, treatment cannot be justified. In this chapter, experts debate the most effective treatments for all eating disorders, including anorexia nervosa.

"Therapists should consider involuntary hospitalization if a client's anorexia-related behaviors are severe enough to suggest that the individual's life is in jeopardy."

Involuntary Treatment of Anorexics Is Justified

James L. Werth Jr. et al.

Eating-disorder experts agree that anorexia nervosa is exceptionally difficult to treat because anorexics do not want, and actively resist, treatment. In the following viewpoint, psychologist James L. Werth Jr. and colleagues argue that medical professionals have a duty to protect that justifies involuntary anorexia treatment, including hospitalization and forced feeding, because the disorder is deadly, anorexics' decision-making abilities and judgment are impaired, and anorexics pose a substantial harm to themselves. James L. Werth Jr. is an associate professor in the Department of Psychology at the University of Akron in Ohio and a writer on end-of-life and HIV issues.

James L. Werth Jr. et al., "When Does the 'Duty to Protect' Apply with a Client Who Has Anorexia Nervosa?" *Counseling Psychologist*, vol. 31, no. 4, July 2003, pp. 427–50. Copyright © 2003 by the Division 17 of Counseling Psychology of the American Psychological Association. Reproduced by permission of Sage Publications.

As you read, consider the following questions:

1. How does anorexia affect a sufferer's cognitive functioning, according to Werth and his colleagues?

2. According to the authors, why is strong intervention justified even if the anorexia patient is not explicitly suicidal?

3. How do the authors counter the arguments that involuntary hospitalization violates the anorexia patient's autonomy?

Individuals with eating disorders, especially those with anorexia nervosa, have the potential to experience significant harm and even death as a result of behaviors related to their condition. Because of this risk, [we] argue that there is a duty to protect (i.e., an obligation to take some action when a person is engaging or considering engaging in a behavior that may lead to self-harm) when a client's anorexia-related behavior has progressed to the point of medical jeopardy—that is, her or his life is in danger. . . .

Anorexia Impairs Cognitive Functioning

The *DSM-IV-TR* [*Diagnostic and Statistical Manual of Mental Disorders*] is silent about how anorexia can affect cognitive functioning beyond mentioning comorbid mental disorders. Experts on anorexia have noted that self-starvation can interfere with conceptualization, perceptions, and decision making. These cognitive deficits can impact the person's ability to realistically assess her situation and then impair judgment to the point that she is legally incompetent, specifically in areas related to eating and receiving treatments designed to increase weight and/or become medically stable. [According to E. Goldner] "The question of competence for individuals with anorexia nervosa centers on their specific ability to make rational decisions about nutrition, refeeding, and other medical treatments." In other words, the disorder itself impairs judgment.

Because they are often high functioning in other areas, the lack of severe delusions or other psychotic features in these clients can deceive some clinicians, attorneys, and judges. Depending on the course of the condition, these deficits may be apparent in standardized psychological and neuropsychological testing. In more severe cases, the inability to care for self as well as the person's medical jeopardy will be evident to observers.

Although not a cognitive deficit in and of itself, the pattern of thinking by the person with anorexia can be considered to be a thought disturbance. Importantly, it is the ego-syntonic dimension of this thought disturbance that negatively affects help seeking, treatment compliance, and retention in therapy. Despite their obvious physiological decline, these clients refuse to acknowledge the extent of their disorder and are secretly pleased with their emaciation. Unlike those with other conditions, clients with anorexia value and seek the symptoms of their disorder (i.e., thinness and starvation). Because clients with anorexia rely on and value their symptoms to organize and manage their lives, there is little or no incentive for change, especially given their almost delusional capacity to ignore their emaciation. There is, then, a synergy between the ego-syntonic dimension of the disorder and the physiological-cognitive response to starvation. These cognitive factors create a reinforcing loop that fuels and maintains the need for personal control, to control food intake, and to resist change (and therefore treatment).

Anorexia Is Deadly

The *DSM-IV-TR* indicates that the long-term mortality for individuals with anorexia admitted to university hospitals is 10%; death usually results from the effects of starvation, an electrolyte imbalance, or suicide. These conclusions were likely based on several studies and reviews that have been conducted in the past 20 years on the causes and rate of mortality of

Anorexics Appreciate, Not Resent, Involuntary Treatment

Involuntary care can be compassionate care. Although accounts remain sparse in the literature, several recent publications have reported that anorexia nervosa patients who are treated involuntarily do as well in acute treatment as "voluntary" patients. In sum, after treatment, they offer a grudging or overt "thank you" rather than wishing "a plague on you."

[Research by Angela S. Guarda et al.] contributes substantially to supporting the practice of using perceived coercion or frank pressure to be admitted in order to treat severely ill eating disorder patients. The study illustrates how short-term beneficence trumps autonomy in selected situations and how quickly autonomy is restored with treatment. Within several weeks of the start of treatment, the ego-syntonic nature [self-image strongly bound to the eating disorder] diminishes, yielding to the patient's recognition of the need for treatment and autonomous of treatment.

Arnold Anderson, "Eating Disorders and Coercion,"
American Journal of Psychiatry, *vol. 164,*
January 2007, pp. 9 11.

those who exhibit the condition. After reviewing this research, [P.F.] Sullivan (1995) recounted this list of comparisons:

The aggregate annual mortality rate associated with anorexia nervosa is more than 12 times higher than the annual death rate due to all causes of death for females 15–24 years old in the general population . . . and more than 200 times greater than the suicide rate in the general population. . . . The annual mortality rate associated with anorexia nervosa is more than twice that of a national study group of female psychiatric patients.

This led Sullivan to conclude, "These data highlight the status of anorexia as a serious psychiatric disorder with a substantial risk of mortality.". . .

Is There a Duty to Protect Clients Who Have Anorexia?

The preceding discussion . . . leads to the following key points:

- Anorexia is a diagnosable mental condition in both the *DSM-IV-TR* and the *ICD-10* (World Health Organization, 1992).

- People with anorexia have a high mortality rate because of medical complications associated with the disorder and because of suicide.

- An ethical duty to protect exists when a client is a potential harm-to-self (although the actual intervention is dependent on the standard of care for that clinical situation).

- The APA [American Psychiatric Association] (2002) ethics code permits the breaking of confidentiality to protect a person from self-harm.

- Possibilities exist for involuntary hospitalization of a person whose self-harm is not necessarily intentional but is the result of a mental disorder or grave disability.

- Involuntarily hospitalized persons can refuse treatment unless declared incompetent. It is in this context that the counselor may be faced with the clinical, ethical, and legal dilemma of how to protect a client with anorexia from the life-threatening impact of the disorder while maintaining the client's autonomy (which is especially significant given that control typically is such an important issue for individuals with eating disorders).

If a client with anorexia is explicitly suicidal, then a duty to protect likely exists. However, the issue . . . is the broader one of whether the eating-related behaviors associated with anorexia nervosa *in and of themselves* activate the duty to protect. In other words, . . . we are *not* saying that client behaviors associated with severe anorexia amount to suicidality but rather that the client's disorder-related actions may at some point put her health at significant risk and this is what engenders the duty to protect. . . .

Involuntary Hospitalization

[P.S.] Appelbaum and [T.] Rumpf discussed the prospect of involuntary hospitalization for people with anorexia. These authors explicitly stated that civil commitment in the case of anorexia is analogous to "other areas of mental health practice, involving the treatment of overtly suicidal patients or those so gravely disabled as to be unable to meet their basic needs." Yet the authors noted that it appears rare for people with anorexia to be involuntarily hospitalized, perhaps because many therapists do not consider a client with anorexia, who is not explicitly suicidal, to be a harm-to-self and, therefore, do not consider attempting involuntary hospitalization if other interventions fail. However, as previously reviewed, neither overt suicidality nor intent to harm oneself is necessary for the duty to protect to apply. Furthermore, given the mortality data previously cited, it should be clear that

> the effect of anorexic behavior can be fully as lethal as the more direct suicidal actions of a severely depressed patient. Thus, the focus on expressed intent is misleading and potentially harmful to the patient. . . . Even without the intent to end their lives, anorexics often act in ways that make that outcome likely.

As a result, Appelbaum and Rumpf concluded, therapists should consider involuntary hospitalization if a client's anorexia-related behaviors are severe enough to suggest that the individual's life is in jeopardy.

Although a few authors have made the case that some individuals with anorexia may be acting in ways, or have progressed far enough in their disease process, to warrant strong interventions, others object to the consideration of involuntary treatment for these clients. Reasons most often cited include potential violation of client rights, questionable efficacy of enforced treatment, and the likely deterioration of the therapeutic relationship.

One of the primary concerns regarding the use of involuntary hospitalization or compulsory treatment is that this imposition violates the client's right to decide for herself—her autonomy is taken away. This violation of client rights is seen as running counter to good therapeutic practice and believed to be counterproductive in both the short and long run. Although this may be true in principle, experts in anorexia indicate that clients are often grateful for such intervention once they are not in the downward spiral of the disorder.

Experts have also suggested that involuntary hospitalization serves the temporary purpose of medical stabilization but does not actually treat the eating disorder because this requires the cooperation of the client. Although short-term results are positive, the long-term success rates of involuntary treatment have been less clear. Only three studies to date have assessed the outcome of involuntary treatment. . . . All three indicated that the involuntary patients experienced successful refeeding, although the results took longer than with the voluntary patients (mean 113 days compared to mean 88 days, respectively). Long-term follow-up was not done, but mortality comparisons were made with the London data. At an average of 5.7 years post-admission, the involuntary patients had a higher mortality rate (10 of 70 involuntary patients had died compared with 2 of the 70 voluntary patients). This was believed to be the result of the more severe pathology of the involuntary patients. How many deaths were prevented by the hospitalization, however, is unknown. More research is required to determine the long-term therapeutic impact of involuntary hospitalization.

Another concern about involuntary treatments is that such efforts could irreparably damage the therapeutic relationship and make it less likely that the client would seek treatment in the future. There are no data to suggest that this is true, however, and some authors offer anecdotal evidence that clients are more likely to be grateful for the intervention once they are medically and psychologically stable. . . .

The risk factors listed below indicate more protective/ aggressive treatment strategies are necessary, which may include behavioral contracts, intensive outpatient treatment, and, ultimately, voluntary or involuntary hospitalization.

High-risk indicators include

1. BMI below 15 (e.g., 5'2" and 82 pounds [5.8 stone]; 5'5" and 90 pounds [6.4 stone]; 5'8" and 98 pounds [7 stone])

2. Any of the following medical conditions: cardiac arrhythmia, seizures, syncopol episodes, organic brain syndrome, bradycardia (less than 40 bpm), exercise-induced chest pain, reduced exercise tolerance, dysrhythmias, renal dysfunction, tetany, blood volume depletion

3. Abnormalities in electrolyte levels

4. Rapid weight loss into dangerous weight range for height

5. Comorbid psychiatric conditions (e.g., major depression, obsessive-compulsive disorder, bipolar disorder, post-traumatic stress disorder, substance abuse)

6. History of self-harm or prior hospitalizations

7. Cognitive impairment that interferes with judgment to the point that the person is incompetent or gravely disabled . . .

The Therapist Has the Duty to Protect

To practice up to the standard of care when working with clients who are at risk of self-harm, psychologists must take some action to protect the person. We have asserted that when a counselor is seeing a client with anorexia, the therapist may eventually have a duty to take action to protect the client's health even if the client is not explicitly suicidal and is not engaging in anorexic behaviors with the explicit intent of self-harm. The specific diagnosis is not the key; the behaviors associated with the diagnosis are what trigger the duty. For example, just as a diagnosis of major depression does not automatically require intervention to protect the well-being of the client unless the behaviors or potential behaviors associated with the depression (e.g., suicidal ideation with a plan or attempt) signaled that significant harm was believed likely, the diagnosis of anorexia in and of itself is not sufficient. However, if the behaviors associated with the condition are such that the therapist, after medical consultation, perceives the client's life to be in danger, then the duty would apply. . . .

At times, there is a duty to protect with clients who have anorexia nervosa. The medical danger associated with this condition invokes the ethical and legal responsibility to protect clients in an acute state of the disorder. Counseling psychologists and trainees would benefit from an increased understanding of the overlap of clinical and ethical dimensions of decision making and treatment planning with clients with anorexia. We hope that this article will prompt others to examine this issue and that researchers will work to further define the conditions under which the duty to protect applies. Until then, counselors are reminded that even if their clients with anorexia nervosa are not explicitly suicidal, the behaviors associated with this condition do put these clients at risk of significant self-harm and death, and the therapist therefore may have an affirmative duty to protect clients with anorexia.

> *"People with anorexia nervosa, who competently decide not to be artificially fed, should be respected because everybody is entitled to exercise their autonomy."*

Some Anorexics Have the Right to Refuse Treatment

Simona Giordano

Even though anorexia is not unavoidable or irreversible like debilitating chronic or terminal illnesses, bioethicist Simona Giordano argues in the following viewpoint that competent anorexics have the same ethical and legal right to refuse medical treatment that terminally ill people have. Involuntary treatment, Giordano maintains, violates individual autonomy and may only prolong suffering. Simona Giordano is a lecturer in bioethics at the School of Law and director of undergraduate medical ethics teaching at the School of Medicine, University of Manchester, England.

As you read, consider the following questions:

1. When is an anorexic's refusal of medical treatment a competent decision, according to Giordano?

2. What are the five cases in which an anorexic's refusal of treatment should be respected, according to bioethicist Heather Draper?

3. In the author's view, when should therapists consider a person's request to refuse anorexia treatment out of pity?

[B]ioethicist Heather] Draper points out that '[t]here may be circumstances under which a sufferer's refusal of consent to treatment should be respected. This argument will hinge upon whether someone in the grip of an eating disorder can actually make a *competent decision about the quality of life*.'

To evaluate the plausibility of this claim, it is first necessary to delineate the notion of 'competence', and then to look at clinical analyses of eating disordered behaviour.

Competence Justifies Treatment Refusal

'Competence' is a task specific concept, that is, a person may be able to make a competent decision at one time, but not at another, or they may, at the same time, be able to make one decision but not another. Moreover, competence is independent of the result of the choice. People are acknowledged to have the right to be unwise and wrong, to refuse treatment for reasons which are irrational, unreasonable, or for no reason at all. People are considered competent to make a medical decision when they are able *to understand the nature and purpose of treatment, and to weigh its risks and benefits*. Moreover, [according to Draper] 'being classed as suffering from a mental illness is [not] necessarily an indication that one is an incompetent individual'; for example, in the case of a prisoner with a diagnosis of personality disorders who refused food, coercive feeding was deemed unlawful, because, despite the ongoing mental disorder, he was found competent to refuse that treatment. . . .

We should not conclude that all people with anorexia are necessarily incompetent to refuse treatment. On the contrary, [according to Draper] we should 'be open to the possibility that sufferers are actually *as competent as anyone else* to make decisions about the quality of their lives, and to assess the relative value of their lives in the light of its quality.' Draper asks:

> [W]hat of the sufferer from anorexia who refuses therapy, not because she thinks that her condition is not life-threatening, nor because she refuses to accept that she has a problem at all, but because for her [...] the burden of therapy and the side-effects of successful therapy—in terms of the body with which she will be left—are such that she prefers to take her chances with death?

According to Draper, a person with anorexia nervosa is competently refusing artificial feeding when she decides 'to withdraw from therapy not on the grounds that she didn't want to eat, nor that she was "fat" but because the quality of her life was so poor that the therapy was no longer of benefit to her, or that it was on balance more of a burden than benefit.'

In other words, the sufferer may be unable to manage with food; however, she may still be able to decide that she is no longer willing to live under conditions such as these. She may therefore be incompetent at the level of diet management, but competent at the level of medical decisions. At this level, in fact, she may *possess all necessary information* about herself and the quality of her life, and may be *able to use* it to arrive at a choice. It may be on the grounds of her considerations about herself and the quality of her life that she may refuse therapy.

The refusal of artificial feeding may thus be considered as a competent decision if the sufferer is able to judge the quality of her life and when she founds her decision on such a judgement, rather than on the basis of her fears and cognitive dysfunctions. This probably only concerns a 'tiny minority' of sufferers, but this does not mean that they do not deserve our moral respect.

The problems that I shall discuss from now onward do not relate to this characterisation of competence, which is perfectly acceptable, but to the arguments that follow this characterisation.

Autonomy Justifies Treatment Refusal

From the above arguments we understand that . . . if someone in the grip of anorexia is able to make a competent decision about the quality of her life, and, in the light of this judgement, decides not to be treated, her refusal of treatment should be respected. . . .

In cases of debilitating chronic and terminal illnesses, the respect for the patient's decision [to refuse treatment] is supported not only by the principle of respect for competent decisions (an application of the principle of autonomy that is widely accepted both in morality and in law). In these cases, the fact that the *condition* is *irreversible* and (in terminal illnesses) premature *death* is *unavoidable* represent additional moral reasons for respecting the patient's competent decision. Because of these additional moral reasons, the respect for the patient's request of omission or withdrawal from life-saving therapy is (relatively) less controversial than the respect for a similar request, when the patient does not suffer from a similar condition.

In anorexia nervosa . . . strictly speaking the condition is not *irreversible*, and death is not *unavoidable*. Therefore these additional moral reasons are lacking. Consequently, it seems that the competent refusal of life-saving or life-prolonging treatment can be respected only on the grounds that people are entitled to make competent decisions about their life (and its termination) (principle of autonomy).

Anorexic Patients and Their Parents Speak Out Against Involuntary Treatment

"If you give compulsory treatment when the condition is chronic, then you're just—prolonging the inevitable. If you give treatment when the condition is in it's early stages, middle stages, then you are prolonging the time they can get well." (Mother G)

"Everybody should have the right to choose whether they want to live or die, it's not fair that they should take away the choice from them."(Daughter B) . . .

"If someone's had the illness for years and years and they've been you know, and in that sort of case they don't want to live, maybe, and it's been tried and they've been [hospitalized] lots of times before, they've been 'tubed' [with a naso-gastric tube] and they just keep going, then maybe I think they should be left." (Daughter D)

"I think if someone is going to starve themselves to the point where they are dying, then . . . I think that to get to that stage, it's something that they want to do, and we should not stand in their way. Because if you say to them, 'okay, it's up to you, you do it [or], you don't do it,' then it's in their hands. And I think to take away that right, is morally wrong. It's morally wrong, to keep someone alive when they don't want to be. If you can't live to be eating, you should be allowed to die with it. You can't die in horrible circumstances, you must be allowed to die quietly, kindly." (Mother G)

Jacinta O.A. Tan et al.,
"Control and Compulsory Treatment in Anorexia Nervosa:
The Views of Patients and Parents,"
International Journal of Law Psychiatry, *vol. 26, no. 6,*
September 2003, pp. 627–45.

This is what I call *the brave claim*: people with anorexia nervosa, who competently decide not to be artificially fed, should be respected *because* everybody is entitled to exercise their autonomy, not only 'in the middle' of their life, but also at the end of it, or when their own life is at stake. The principle of autonomy binds us to respect people's competent decisions about their life and its termination, precisely because autonomy extends also to the most difficult moments of our life, and, ultimately, [as Milan Kundera writes] 'stretches [. . .] far out into the distance' at the end of it. . . .

Instead of making such a claim . . . Draper has tried . . . to demonstrate that *in some cases* this decision is on a par with the decision to refuse treatment in cases of debilitating chronic or terminal illnesses. We should now focus on *these cases*.

The *cases* are the following:

> Where those who are refusing have been afflicted beyond the natural cycle of the disorder (which is between one and eight years); have already been force-fed on previous occasions; are competent to make decisions concerning their quality of life; have insight into the influence which their anorexia has over some aspects of their lives, and are not at death's door (they may, for instance, have just been released from a section for compulsory treatment). . . .

In fact, coercive treatment represents a failure to respect competent refusal of therapy not only *in these cases*, but *every time competent refusal of therapy is not respected.* . . .

Respect Treatment Refusal Out of Compassion and Pity

There is also another aspect of the problem that we should not neglect. In some cases, people with anorexia literally cross the border of humanity. With their skeleton-like bodies, they survive their emaciation, while suffering, sometimes for years, the severe side effects of malnutrition. Whereas the majority of sufferers, sooner or later, recover or at least get much better, a minority of sufferers never seem to get better, and there might be a point at which further therapeutic attempts seem to condemn them to agony. From this point of view, I think it makes sense to consider how many years the person has been ill, and how many attempts she has made to recover. After many years and many therapeutic attempts, and after many reiterated competent requests for suspension of therapy, I believe we should probably consider the patient's request, not necessarily because the person is now *more competent* than before, but, more probably, *out of pity.* . . .

It would be inappropriate to provide general guidelines that tell people how they should behave in these circumstances. However, I believe that carers should be encouraged to consider all aspects of the problem. Among those aspects, we should also include the condition and the suffering of the person who refuses therapy. Understanding the condition and the suffering of the person with anorexia involves not only a critical attitude toward the situation, but also *compassion* (in its etymological meaning: *com-* with + *pati*—to bear, suffer). Identification with the patient and participation in her suffering may clearly be burdensome for carers. However, compassion enables us to give the patient a genuine understanding and to cultivate a refined sensitivity, more attentive to the peculiar aspects of each individual case, and therefore is essential in order to consider the sufferer's request not to be artificially fed and hydrated.

| *"Family therapy is acceptable, feasible, and effective."*

Family Therapy Is the Most Promising Treatment for Anorexia

James Lock

James Lock is associate professor of child psychiatry and pediatrics at Stanford University School of Medicine, where he directs the eating disorder program in child psychiatry. He is coauthor of the books Treatment Manual for Anorexia Nervosa: A Family-Based Approach *and* Help Your Teenager Beat an Eating Disorder. *In the following viewpoint, Lock criticizes traditional anorexia treatments that intentionally exclude or minimize family involvement. On the contrary, he maintains that family-based treatment (FBT), pioneered at the Maudsley Hospital in London, is superior to individual therapy for adolescent anorexics: Studies show that parental involvement and training effectively promotes immediate weight gain and maintains recovery four to five years after hospitalization.*

James Lock, "The Role of Family Therapy for Adolescents with Anorexia Nervosa (Care and Treatment)," *Psychiatric Times*, vol. 23, no. 10, September 1, 2006, p. 46. Copyright © 2006 by CMP Media, 300 Boston Post Road, Darien, CT 06820, USA. Reprinted with permission.

As you read, consider the following questions:

1. According to the author, what are the harmful effects of excluding the family from anorexia treatment programs?

2. In a family-based or Maudsley treatment program, what should parents do to promote their child's weight gain, according to the author?

3. What factors does Lock say increase the likelihood that family-based treatment will be successful?

Anorexia nervosa (AN) is a serious psychiatric condition with a prevalence estimated at 0.48% to 0.7% among adolescent females aged 15 to 19 years. Comorbid psychological conditions are also common in patients with AN. Some 60% of patients with eating disorders have a lifetime anxiety or affective disorder. The mortality rates associated with this severely disabling condition are higher than for any other psychiatric disorder, with about half of the deaths occurring from suicide and the remainder as a result of the physical complications of AN. In addition, AN is an expensive illness to treat, with costs comparable to those for schizophrenia.

Family therapy, one of the few treatments for AN that has been systematically examined, may show the most promise, especially for adolescent patients. The inclusion of parents in their children's treatment for eating disorder is not universally accepted, particularly when parents are encouraged to make strong behavioral interventions. However, recent studies suggest that families should be included in treatment and that they are often a powerful resource for helping their children recover.

"Worst Attendants" or Partners in Recovery?

The role of families in the management of AN has been controversial from the earliest medical descriptions of the disorder. William Gull called families the "worst attendants" and J.M. Charcot referred to parents as a pernicious influence on their offspring with AN. The clinical recommendation arising from these observations was to remove the parents from involvement in their child's care in a maneuver sometimes called parentectomy. Other experts have justified excluding or minimally involving families when treatment targets the individual developmental needs of adolescents, including autonomy, assertiveness, and self-control.

In contrast, Salvador Minuchin and colleagues found that family involvement in treatment appeared to benefit young patients with AN, albeit with a focus primarily on ameliorating family pathology related to rigidity, enmeshment, conflict avoidance, and overprotectiveness. It was left to Christopher Dare and Ivan Eisler and their colleagues at the Maudsley Hospital in London to develop a family treatment protocol that used families as a therapeutic resource to enhance recovery for adolescent AN.

The Birth of FBT

Family-based treatment (FBT), sometimes called the Maudsley method or Maudsley approach, is a treatment that was inspired by Minuchin's findings that families could be an asset in treating youngsters with AN. Dare and Eisler also recognized that inpatient weight restoration in the hands of competent staff often set the stage for recovery. They believed that parents, with appropriate guidance and encouragement, could provide the support at home, thus avoiding hospitalization.

As a result, Dare and Eisler developed an outpatient therapeutic approach to help parents disrupt extreme dieting and exercise in their children. Their program aimed to assist parents in normalizing their children's eating and weight in a way similar to what is done in an expert inpatient eating disorder unit. A manual detailing this approach has been published and used in both clinical and research settings. A parent guide has also been written to support parents in learning about this form of family treatment.

Treatment Protocols

Early in FBT, parents are helped to understand the medical and psychiatric seriousness of AN, including the high mortality rates because of cardiac failure and suicide. Although this information raises parental anxiety, the therapist uses this information to show parents that they are a crucial resource in preventing devastating outcomes.

Parents are encouraged to find solutions to the problems of food refusal and weight loss–inducing behaviors. Usually this entails helping the parents agree on a strategy to increase the amounts and types of food their child is eating and to limit the child's physical activity. Thus, in the first part of the FBT program, parents learn to get organized, become consistent, and be persistent without getting angry and frustrated with their child.

At the beginning of treatment, FBT is highly focused on eliminating food refusal and promoting weight gain. Issues related to family or individual processes are deferred unless they directly interfere with weight restoration. Once weight is restored and the adolescent is eating more regularly, control of eating is returned to the adolescent. After the adolescent demonstrates sufficient ability to eat normally and maintain a normal weight, therapy turns to more general issues of adolescent development and family process.

The major innovation of putting parents in control of weight restoration sets FBT apart from other therapies for AN. Like parents of children with autism, schizophrenia, and other illnesses, parents of children with AN have long felt blamed, responsible, and guilty for their children's illness. As a result, they felt powerless to help their children.

FBT aims to diminish these sentiments and powerlessness in several ways. First, parents are reminded that there is no known cause for AN. The approach further empowers parents by encouraging them to directly challenge and disrupt the severe dieting and overexercise associated with AN as they would

The Maudsley Approach: Pioneering Family Therapy for Anorexia

The Maudsley approach involves the family from the outset of treatment and relies heavily on parent involvement in the re-feeding of the child with an eating disorder.

A unique aspect of this approach is that families are not thought to be pathological in the etiology of the eating disorder. Parents are exonerated from blame. Their creative resources and strengths are drawn on to move their child toward health. . . .

In the Maudsley approach parents are empowered to use their resources and creativity to figure out ways to feed their child the type and amounts of food needed to restore health. However, once health is reasonably restored (determined by medical indicators such as achieving 95% of ideal weight) the model returns responsibility for re-feeding back to the adolescent. At that point, the adolescent in treatment is presumed to be ready to undertake the age-appropriate adolescent task of self-feeding. . . .

The responsibility for re-feeding a child, while empowering for parents, is also labor-intensive and time-consuming. Parents, like the nursing staff in an inpatient setting, are "on duty" all day for feedings, including snacks. While parents may tag-team each other for meals and snacks, at least one parent or guardian needs to be present for all planned snacks and meals. Applications for bulimic behavior may include purge-prevention supervision, as well, as worked out with the therapist. Parent and/or guardian at-home "teams" need to be able to work in unity and to cooperate with each other.

Cris Haltom, "The Maudsley Approach,"
Eating Disorder Survival Guide for Parents, *2004.*
www.edsurvivalguide.com/eatingdisorder-maudsley.htm.

any other dangerous adolescent behavior (e.g., alcohol or drug use, truancy, or recklessness). The issue of adolescent control is reformulated to help parents see that extreme dieting and the resulting malnutrition are evidence that their child needs help and should not be left to his or her own devices regarding eating behavior.

What the Studies Show

There are only 5 randomized controlled outpatient trials of psychological treatment for adolescents with AN. These trials were conducted over the past 20 years and comprised about 200 participants. All of these trials involved FBT in some form. Taken together, these studies suggest that family therapy is acceptable, feasible, and effective. In fact, dropout rates were modest (between 10% and 15%), in contrast to treatment studies of adults with AN, where dropout rates of 40% or more effectively made randomized outcomes difficult to analyze and interpret. Outcomes of adolescents in these studies suggest that between 70% and 80% do well in FBT in terms of weight restoration, normalization of eating-related thoughts and behaviors, and psychosocial functioning. In comparison, outcomes in adult studies report 30% to 40% recovery rates.

Studies comparing FBT with other approaches are few and small in scale. Although the results available suggest that FBT may be superior in adolescent participants, definitive conclusions about comparative outcomes await further study. Interestingly, studies of adults with AN who were treated with FBT are less convincing; in such cases, FBT may be no better than individual therapy.

Long-term outcomes of adolescent patients treated with FBT suggest that the improvements obtained during treatment are enduring. Two studies have demonstrated that both weight restoration and eating-related thoughts and behaviors continue to be improved at follow-up 4 to 5 years later. However, although the majority of these adolescents have recovered from their eating disorder and are working or are in school, about a quarter of them have other mental health problems, including depression and anxiety disorders.

Because of the high cost of managing AN, one of the more exciting findings is that FBT can be a remarkably efficient therapy. In its chronic form, AN is highly intractable to known interventions, often requiring long-term and intensive interventions. However, many younger and less chronically ill adolescent patients appear to respond favorably with the relatively short treatment protocols of family therapy.

Based on a review of existing studies of FBT for adolescents with AN, the duration of treatment ranged from 6 months to 18 months, with most treatment durations falling between 6 months and 12 months. Intensity of treatment (number of sessions provided during the treatment period) ranged from 9 sessions to 31 sessions over a 12-month period. . . . Outcome did not appear to vary as a result of the intensity or duration of treatment, since participants who were treated for as few as 9 sessions over 6 months did as well as those who were treated for 47 sessions over 18 months. . . .

However, for patients with severe obsessions and compulsions related to eating behaviors or for those who came from nonintact families, longer treatment appeared to be more effective. Overall, the findings of this study provide substantive support that a brief course of treatment is as effective as a longer course in adolescents who are treated with FBT. These results highlight the advantage of employing parents in FBT not only in terms of promoting recovery but also clinical efficiency and cost-effectiveness.

Two studies have examined patient and family views of FBT. Both studies found that patients and families thought FBT was helpful and successful, but approximately one-third of the adolescents in one study reported a desire for individual treatment in addition to FBT. These studies suggest, somewhat surprisingly given the ego-syntonic nature of AN [anorexia is an important part of patients' self-concept or identity], that adolescents as well as their parents not only accept FBT but also develop strong therapeutic relationships with the therapist.

For example, in one study, early patient therapeutic alliance in FBT facilitated early weight gain, and early parental therapeutic alliance helped prevent dropping out of treatment. There is another noteworthy finding: the study found early weight gain was a better predictor of end of treatment psychological recovery and of end of treatment therapeutic alliance than early therapeutic alliance. This underscores the importance of early behavioral response both to the process of therapeutic engagement and to ultimate outcome in FBT for adolescent AN.

FBT appears to work best with adolescents who have uncomplicated, short-duration AN. Comorbid psychiatric illness and family problems appear to increase dropout rates as well as decrease response rates. Although systematic studies of the mechanisms of the therapeutic action of FBT have yet to be conducted, improvement in comorbid psychiatric symptoms and family pathology early in treatment is associated with increased response rates. In addition, as is common with many treatments for eating disorders, early response, such as weight gain in a patient with AN, also increases the likelihood that the patient will recover.

Two studies have also found that FBT can be delivered in a separated form, wherein the parents are seen separately from their child for therapy focused on weight restoration. This form of FBT may be preferable in cases in which there is a high degree of overt criticism (e.g., high levels of expressed emotion) of the child.

Future Directions

Since Dare and Eisler's first published studies of FBT more than 20 years ago, a collection of both uncontrolled and controlled studies have been conducted using this approach. Although none of these studies are definitive, together they produce considerable evidence in support of FBT for adolescent AN. This has been recognized in the National Institute for Clinical Excellence in the United Kingdom evidence-based practice report, in the Agency for Healthcare Research and Quality recommendations and, most recently, in the new practice guidelines for the treatment of eating disorders by the American Psychiatric Association.

Nonetheless, there is a clear need for more definitive comparative studies. Funded by the National Institutes of Health, a randomized controlled trial comparing FBT to a developmentally tailored individual treatment for adolescents with AN is currently under way at the University of Chicago and Stanford University. Studies comparing FBT to other forms of family therapy for AN in adolescents are being initiated in other centers, including Cornell University, Washington University, Lauriette Psychiatric Clinic and Hospital, Sheppard Pratt Health System, and the University of Toronto. We hope that these larger-scale studies will identify the best treatments, as well as help to determine the best therapy for each individual.

New directions for studying FBT include assessing the utility of the approach for adolescents with bulimia nervosa, evaluating FBT's effects on young adults living at home or with relatives, as well as assessing the integration of the approach in more intensive treatment settings such as day programs, intensive outpatient programs, and inpatient programs. Other therapy formats, particularly family group formats, are also being developed.

A particular challenge common to many evidence-based treatments is efficient and effective dissemination of the approach to clinicians in practice. Training professionals and future professionals in FBT remains a limiting factor in making this approach available to patients outside of specialty centers.

The long-standing controversy concerning whether parents should be involved in the treatment of their adolescent children with AN appears to be resolving. The studies of family treatment conducted thus far clearly support actively including parents in the treatment of their adolescent children with AN. Parents and other family members are an important resource, especially for these younger patients in crisis. Most important, by using family treatment it appears to be possible to forestall the evolution of more chronic, often intractable, and devastating forms of AN.

| *"There is 'no evidence of any treatments that are effective for chronic anorexia.'"*

There Are No Effective Treatments for Chronic Anorexia

Judith Graham

As journalist Judith Graham writes in the following viewpoint, recent research indicates that neither behavioral therapies nor medications such as antidepressants are effective against chronic anorexia, the term for anorexia recurring into adulthood or lasting three or more years. Unlike bulimia and binge eating disorder, Graham reports, anorexia is considered intractable unless the disorder is diagnosed and aggressively treated early in adolescence. Judith Graham is a staff reporter for the Chicago Tribune *covering news in health, medicine, and science.*

As you read, consider the following questions:

1. According to Graham, what is the relapse rate following hospitalization for anorexia?

2. What neurochemical evidence does Graham cite as a potentially permanent obstacle to anorexia treatment?

3. What treatments have had limited effect in very young anorexia patients, according to the author?

Anorexia nervosa has a disturbing distinction in the field of mental health: It's the most lethal of all disorders. A key reason is the lack of effective treatments for this condition, which causes teenagers to obsess over their weight and severely restrict the food they eat.

About 3 million Americans, mostly girls and young women, struggle with anorexia; the mortality rate for this illness is 10 percent to 15 percent.

Two [2006] reports confirm the sobering challenges faced by patients and medical practitioners.

In April, a comprehensive scientific review found that medications don't help people with anorexia and that behavioral therapies offer limited benefits.

The eating-disorders study was prepared for the federal Agency for Healthcare Research and Quality.

"These findings underscore the need to learn more about the causes of these frightening and poorly understood illnesses," said Dr. Carolyn Clancy, who directs the government agency.

A study in the [June 2006] *Journal of the American Medical Association* [JAMA] sounds a similar theme. It concludes that the anti-depressant Prozac isn't effective in preventing relapses in anorexic patients who had attained a normal weight.

Relapses are a major problem with this illness.

While inpatient hospital programs help young women put on extra pounds, those gains typically disappear when people leave the hospital, and as many as 50 percent of patients require re-hospitalization.

In the *JAMA* report, 53 of 93 patients in Toronto and New York City who entered the study dropped out because their condition deteriorated significantly.

Conventional Anorexia Treatments May Even Exacerbate the Disorder

[Gender studies professor Helen] Gremillion reveals how therapies participate unwittingly in ideals of gender, individualism, physical fitness and family life that have contributed to the dramatic increase in the incidence of anorexia in the United States since the 1970s.

She describes how treatment strategies, which include the meticulous measurement of patients' progress in terms of body weight and calories consumed, ultimately feed the problem, not only reinforcing ideas about the regulation of women's bodies, but also fostering in many girls and women greater expertise in the skills anorexia requires.

"The patients in the program I studied are required to have an exact calorie count every day. There is also detailed attention to even very small weight gains and losses," Gremillion said. "Of course, any treatment program must devise ways to encourage eating and weight gain, but I argue that such careful attention to the numbers plays right into anorexia's hands. The focus of the treatment takes on a life of its own to the extent that it ends up reinforcing the problem."

Indiana University Bloomington, Media Relations,
"Procedures Can Reinforce What They Try to Remedy,"
review of Helen Gremillion, Feeding Anorexia:
Gender and Power at a Treatment Center,
September 16, 2003.

The remaining 40 patients received 50 sessions of cognitive behavior therapy and either Prozac or a dummy pill. There was no evidence the drug produced any benefit compared with the placebo.

Impact of Anti-Depressants

"We've already known for a number of years that anti-depressants aren't useful for underweight patients in the acute phase of the illness," said Dr. B. Timothy Walsh, a professor of psychiatry at Columbia University and lead author of the report. "What we haven't known until now is whether these medications might be helpful once the underweight state is remedied."

There was reason to believe Prozac might work. An earlier clinical trial had shown that patients with bulimia nervosa who took the medication for 16 to 18 weeks were less likely to experience a relapse. Bulimia is a "binge and purge" eating disorder that involves gorging on food and then vomiting.

But anorexia appears to be more intractable than bulimia. That could be because the neurochemistry of the brain is altered when people suffer extreme food deprivation. Imaging studies indicate that the brains of people who suffer from chronic anorexia "aren't normal," said Dr. Allan Kaplan, head of the eating-disorders program at Toronto General Hospital and a co-author of the *JAMA* study.

Changes may be permanent. "A basic question is when someone lives for three or more years in a state of virtual starvation, does that permanently affect brain functioning and impair a person's response to a drug?" Kaplan said. "So far we just don't know."

If anything, the new results underscore the need to get young people with anorexia into treatment as soon as possible, before the illness takes hold. The illness typically strikes teenage girls 15 to 19 years old.

There is "no evidence of any treatments that are effective for chronic anorexia," said Dr. James Lock, director of the eating-disorders program at Packard Children's Hospital at Stanford University.

"By contrast, younger patients in the first few years of the illness do have a good chance of recovery, and you can change the outcome," he said.

"Diagnose the illness early on, use the treatments for which we have evidence, and these kids probably won't become the adults for whom we have such dismal outcomes," said Daniel le Grange, who directs the eating-disorders program at the University of Chicago.

Those treatments include family therapy and certain kinds of individual therapy with collateral sessions for parents. "It takes a long time to change the way these young people think about themselves and food and help them find other ways of dealing with the stresses of life," said Dr. Stephen Galston, medical director of the eating-disorders clinic at Highland Park Hospital.

For clinicians, the major message from the new research is that they shouldn't expect anti-depressants such as Prozac to make much, if any, difference.

Unpublished results from the *JAMA* report indicate that Prozac wasn't effective at treating the underlying anxiety and depression that often accompany this illness, a finding that suggests brain functioning may have been altered, Walsh said. And there is no evidence that medication is effective in younger patients either.

| "Research over more than a decade has shown that medications can indeed be valuable in the treatment of bulimia nervosa."

Medications Effectively Treat Bulimia and Binge-Eating Disorder

Diane Mickley

Although medications have not been shown to be effective against anorexia, psychiatric medications known as selective serotonin reuptake inhibitors (SSRIs) have demonstrated effectiveness against bulimia and binge eating, according to Diane Mickley in the following viewpoint. SSRIs not only counteract brain chemistry imbalances, Mickley argues, but also reduce anxiety, phobias, obsessive-compulsive disorder, and other problems commonly found in people with eating disorders. Diane Mickley is the founder and director of the Wilkins Center for Eating Disorders in Greenwich, Connecticut, and associate clinical professor in the Department of Psychiatry at the Yale University School of Medicine.

As you read, consider the following questions:

1. How do SSRIs work against eating disorders, according to the author?

2. How soon are results apparent in the treatment of bulimia with Prozac, according to Mickley?

3. What adverse side effects of SSRIs does the author consider relatively minor compared with the dangers of eating disorders?

A norexia nervosa and bulimia nervosa are associated with altered levels of neurotransmitters, or chemical messengers in the brain. This is particularly true of serotonin levels. It makes sense, then, that medications developed to improve the function of neurotransmitters might be useful in the treatment of eating disorders. Research over more than a decade has shown that medications can indeed be valuable in the treatment of bulimia nervosa. . . .

SSRIs

Several different categories of psychiatric medications have been shown to be beneficial, but the most widely studied are the SSRIs (Selective Serotonin Reuptake Inhibitors), the first and most famous of which is fluoxetine, or Prozac. Other SS-RIs include sertraline (Zoloft), paroxetine (Paxil), fluvoxamine (Luvox), and citalopram/escitalopram (Celexa/Lexapro). All raise the levels of serotonin available in parts of the brain. Venlafaxine (Effexor) is a related drug that raises both serotonin and norepinephrine.

Though popularly dubbed antidepressants, these drugs are used for a wide array of psychiatric diagnoses, including anxiety, phobias, panic attacks, obsessive-compulsive disorder (OCD), premenstrual dysphoria (PMS), post-traumatic stress disorder (PTSD), and impulse control disorders. Many of these are common additional problems in patients with eating disorders and their families. . . .

Medications in the Treatment of Binge-Eating Disorder

Binge-eating disorder (BED) is a newly defined diagnostic category characterized by recurrent episodes of binge eating not followed by the inappropriate compensatory weight loss behaviors characteristic of bulimia nervosa. BED is usually associated with overweight or obesity and psychopathology. Pharmacotherapy may be a useful component of a multidimensional treatment approach. Although pharmacotherapy research in BED is still in its preliminary stages, some drugs have been shown to be promising agents. . . .

Currently, three main classes of drugs have been studied in double-blind, placebo controlled trials in BED: antidepressants, anti-obesity agents, and anticonvulsants. Serotonin selective reuptake inhibitors (SSRIs) are the best studied medications. Thus, fluoxetine, fluvoxamine, sertraline and citalopram have been shown to modestly but significantly reduce binge eating frequency and body weight in BED over the short term. More recently, the anti-obesity agent sibutramine and the anticonvulsant topiramate have been shown to significantly reduce binge eating behavior and body weight in BED associated with obesity.

J.C. Appolinarion and S.L. McElroy,
"Pharmacological Approaches in the Treatment of
Binge Eating Disorder," Current Drug Targets,
April 2004, pp. 301–307.

Bulimia Nervosa Medications

The initial goal for bulimia nervosa is . . . symptom management—in this case, stopping the binge/purge behaviors. Two treatments have been documented by evidence-based scientific studies to have the best short-term success rates. The first is cognitive behavioral therapy (CBT), and the second is high-dose fluoxetine. Results are roughly comparable, with a suggestion that the two together may be better than either one alone. However, since only a quarter of patients achieve symptom remission with these approaches, further treatment is generally needed.

The largest bulimia nervosa treatment trial in the world documented the benefits of high-dose fluoxetine. This led to approval of fluoxetine by the FDA [Food and Drug Administration] specifically for the treatment of bulimia nervosa. Treatment is recommended to begin and continue at a dose of 60 mg. (The dose of 20 mg commonly used for depression was no better than a placebo.) Bulimics benefit from fluoxetine regardless of whether they are depressed. Moreover, if fluoxetine is going to be helpful, the results will be apparent within 4 weeks. At least one study has shown this to be a successful initial approach when used by primary care providers.

Are other medications in the SSRI category also helpful? Published studies have now shown sertraline to benefit bulimia nervosa at a higher dose range (150 mg). Although clinicians commonly do use other SSRIs for this purpose, the data to assess their benefit and dosage is simply not available. Other classes of antidepressant medications have also been shown to be helpful for the treatment of bulimia nervosa and binge eating disorder.

Topiramate [is] a totally different category of medication that was developed for treating epilepsy. It is now commonly used for migraine headaches, and it is an exciting new option for patients with bulimia nervosa, binge eating disorder, and simple obesity. Studies in patients with these disorders show binge reduction, reduced preoccupation with eating, and weight loss. Topiramate is used in relatively low doses (100–200 mg) for eating disorders and weight loss. Gradual initial dose increases are required to avoid mental sluggishness. Other side effects are common but generally not serious. Patients who are taking hormones, including oral contraceptives, may also require dose adjustment due to interaction with topiramate. Zonisamide is another promising agent in this class.

Side Effects

None of the medications described above have any potential to be addicting. Often their use can be transitional, for several months to a year or two, while recovery progresses and solidifies. However, since eating disorders frequently occur in patients with depression or anxiety disorders, some of these people will benefit from longer-term use of medication.

What about side effects? As in all medical care, doctors must weigh the risks of the treatment compared to the risks of the illness. Fortunately, most of the side effects of the medications used for eating disorders are relatively minor, especially compared to the serious dangers of being anorexic or bulimic. The most frequent side effect of olanzapine is significant sedation, especially at the beginning. The SSRIs may have mild initiation side effects including nausea, headache, fatigue, or insomnia, and less commonly agitation and over-excitement. These often pass within a week or two but they may persist and should always be discussed with the physician. More enduring side effects may include vivid dreams, sweating, and a reduction in sexual interest or performance. Medications that leave the body quickly (paroxetine, escitalopram, and venlafaxine) should be tapered off, since sudden discontinuation can produce flu-like symptoms. Recently, the news media has focused on whether teenagers respond as well and safely to SSRIs as adults do. A small percent of adolescents (and a few adults) experience akathisia while taking common psychiatric drugs. Akathisia is a kind of motor restlessness, a feeling of "jumping out of your skin," which should be reported to your physician. In addition, concerns have been voiced about an increased risk of suicide among children and teens taking SSRIs, even though overall suicide rates have dropped significantly as SSRI use has become widespread. Government agencies are currently evaluating this question.

The exciting overview is that continuing progress is being made in understanding the biology of anorexia nervosa and bulimia nervosa, as well as how medications can help.

> *"Of the identified treatments for BN, empirical support is greatest for cognitive-behavioral therapy (CBT)."*

Cognitive Behavioral Therapy Is an Effective Treatment for Bulimia and Binge-Eating Disorder

Ann M. Schapman-Williams, James Lock, and Jennifer Couturier

In the following viewpoint, researchers Ann M. Schapman-Williams, James Lock, and Jennifer Couturier present evidence that cognitive behavioral therapy (CBT) produced significant improvement in adolescents with bulimia and binge-eating disorder. At the end of four-to-eight-month treatment periods, all of the authors' study participants had stopped purging, over half had completely stopped binge eating, and all reported they had stopped food restriction and excessive exercise. Ann M. Schapman-Williams is affiliated with the Department of Psychology and Sociology, Notre Dame de Namur University, in Belmont, California. James Lock is associate professor of child

Ann M. Schapman-Williams, James Lock, and Jennifer Couturier, "Cognitive-Behavioral Therapy for Adolescents with Binge Eating Syndromes: A Case Series," *International Journal of Eating Disorders*, April 2006, pp. 252–55. Copyright © 2006 by Wiley Periodicals, Inc. This material is used by permission of John Wiley & Sons, Inc.

psychiatry in the Department of Psychiatry and Behavioral Sciences at Stanford University. Jennifer Couturier is a psychiatrist in the Eating Disorders Program for Children and Adolescents, London Health Sciences Centre, in Ontario, Canada.

As you read, consider the following questions:

1. According to the authors, how should cognitive behavioral therapy be adjusted to take into account the developmental differences between adolescents and adults?
2. How did Schapman-Williams, Lock, and Couturier involve patients' parents in the CBT treatment plan?
3. What do the authors identify as the limitations of their pilot study?

The symptoms of bulimia nervosa (BN) often develop during adolescence, yet few studies have assessed the efficacy of psychotherapeutic interventions for these problems in adolescents. Population estimates for BN in adolescents are similar to the estimates for adults, that is, 1%–2% whereas point prevalence rates [based on a single examination at one point in time] for adolescents are approximately 0.5% for girls and 0.3% for boys. However, in addition, many adolescents who present with clinically significant binge eating and purging behaviors do not meet diagnostic thresholds. Many adolescents with binge eating and purging behaviors are diagnosed as having an eating disorder not otherwise specified (EDNOS). Thus, these problematic eating behaviors are more numerous than even the rates reported above suggest.

Clinical data for adolescents with BN syndromes are limited, but reports indicate they are clinically similar to their adult counterparts. Currently, clinicians often turn to the empirical literature conducted with adults with BN to guide their interventions with adolescents. Of the identified treatments for BN, empirical support is greatest for cognitive-behavioral therapy (CBT).

It has been suggested that for CBT to be effective for adolescents, it requires adaptation because of developmental differences between younger participants and adults. For example, young adolescents, because of the relatively recent onset of physical changes associated with puberty and associated weight gain, often have a new focus on weight, shape, and body image, leading many to initiate risky dieting procedures. Unfortunately, many adolescents have little experience and knowledge about safe dieting and have limited judgment about the effects of binge eating and purging on their physical and emotional health. In addition, most adolescents, especially younger ones, need the help of parents in undertaking treatment because parents generally provide behavioral guidelines for them and provide food and mealtime structure for the family. At the same time, adolescents are placing a new emphasis on social relationships with peers outside the family. Adolescent egocentrism and burgeoning hypothetical reasoning can also influence the extent to which CBT can be effective. CBT was adapted taking these developmental differences into account and examined in this pilot study.

Testing CBT in Teens with Binge Eating Disorder

Participants were 7 adolescent females . . . presenting to a university-based eating disorder clinic who were referred for treatment from previous therapists, physicians, or their parents. The sample comprised 6 Caucasian patients and 1 biracial patient (Asian American and Caucasian). Three participants met full criteria for BN using criteria outlined in the 4th ed., text revision of the *Diagnostic and Statistical Manual of Mental Disorders* (*DSM-IV-TR*; Washington, DC: American Psychiatric Association; 2000). All of the remaining patients had symptom profiles consistent with BN, but 1 patient was exclusively a binge eater and 3 other patients did not meet the frequency and/or duration of symptom requirements for binge

How Does Cognitive Behavioral Therapy for Eating Disorders Work?

Every Tuesday Katie [a 27-year-old British woman with a 10-year history of bulimia] goes to her local community mental health centre in Essex for a one-on-one session with a psychotherapist trained in CBT. When her name is called, she goes into the small room, gets out her homework—a food diary, risky situation worksheet, shifting core beliefs worksheet, thought monitoring worksheet and other assorted bits of paper—and the therapist asks her to go through everything she has written down. Where was she when she started to binge? What was she doing? Who was she with? What may have triggered it? How did she feel before/during and afterwards?

There is no couch, no "tell me about your childhood/dreams/father". Barely any mention will be made of her past. Instead, the therapist tries to encourage Katie to rationalise her thoughts now, to see the connection between her feelings and her actions. He tries to recognise unhelpful patterns of behaviour ("I ate a whole loaf of bread, then made myself sick because I felt ugly and fat") and replace these with more realistic or helpful ones ("I don't need to binge. I have other ways of controlling my emotions, like calling a friend or going kickboxing"). This very practical, proactive approach [usually a short course of 5 to 20 hours of therapy] is rather different from the classic modes of therapy, which one CBT convert describes as "frustratingly fluffy and meaningless" and "encouraging you to feel you are not responsible for your own personal wellbeing".

Helen Pidd, "A Little More Conversation,"
Guardian Unlimited *(London), June 30, 2006.*

and purge episodes of the *DSM-IV-TR*. In addition, 1 patient had attention-deficit/hyperactivity disorder, and another had major depressive disorder. In these cases, however, the eating disorder was deemed the most clinically severe problem requiring treatment. . . .

At intake, participants completed clinical interviews that assess current and past eating disorder symptoms. Data regarding the frequency of binge eating and purging behavior obtained during these interviews were utilized in the subsequent analyses. Participants also completed a semistructured interview, the Eating Disorders Examination (EDE), before the start of treatment and at the end of treatment. . . .

All participants completed CBT for BN according to the Fairburn et al. manual adapted for adolescents. Adaptations provided increased attention to the development of a therapeutic relationship with the adolescent, allowed for a greater emphasis on social relationships and interpersonal struggles commonly associated with adolescence, and used cognitive restructuring strategies at a more basic level with more concrete examples consistent with adolescent abilities. Furthermore, the therapist involved the parents in the treatment to set up the environment to reduce triggers for the symptoms of BN, as well as to accompany the adolescent during and after meals to ensure they did not purge at the onset of treatment. This parental monitoring, however, was phased out by the end of treatment. Parents also assisted with meal planning and provided support and encouragement. . . .

Promising Results

Patients received 10–22 treatment sessions lasting 4–8 months.

Data from the pretreatment and posttreatment interviews were assessed using reports of binge eating and purging frequencies reported during each treatment session for the previous month for all 7 patients. These data suggest reductions of >90% for both binge eating and purging (of all types, e.g., vomiting, laxative use) at the end of treatment. In addition, 4 participants (57%) were completely abstinent from binge eating, and 7 (71%) were abstinent from purging at the end of treatment. Four patients (57%) were abstinent from both behaviors at the end of treatment. . . . Restriction and exercise were also assessed before and after treatment. Results indicated that at the pretreatment assessment, 5 patients endorsed food restriction and 3 patients endorsed excessive exercise. At posttreatment, all patients denied restriction or excessive exercise.

Total and subscale scores from the EDE were compared from pretreatment to posttreatment assessments. All of the patients completed pretreatment EDEs, and 4 of the patients completed posttreatment EDEs. Results indicated significant reductions in the total and all subscale scores of the EDE from pretreatment to posttreatment. Specifically, total scores displayed a statistically significant decline from pretreatment to posttreatment. . . .

Results indicated a significant reduction in behavioral, cognitive, and emotional aspects of BN at the end of treatment, including a statistically significant reduction in frequency of binge eating per week from pretreatment to posttreatment and a nearly significant reduction in rates of purging per week. The presence of restriction and overexercise diminished through the course of treatment as well. In addition, even with a small sample, the total score and all subscale scores of the EDE showed significant declines from the pretreatment to the posttreatment assessment. These results are consistent with outcomes in adults treated with CBT, suggesting that CBT may be an effective treatment to reduce the symptoms of BN in adolescents as well.

There are limitations to this pilot study. Most notable are the small sample size and the variation in severity and specific types of symptoms of BN. Recent reports on the clinical simi-

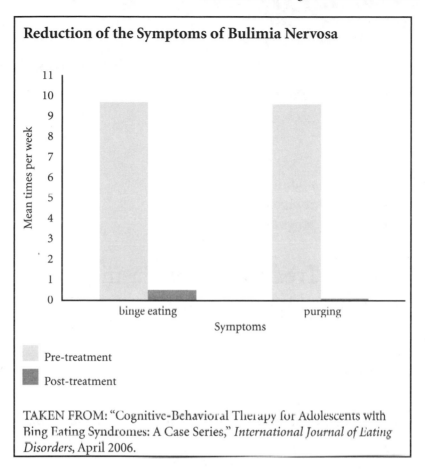

Reduction of the Symptoms of Bulimia Nervosa

Pre-treatment

Post-treatment

TAKEN FROM: "Cognitive-Behavioral Therapy for Adolescents with Bing Eating Syndromes: A Case Series," *International Journal of Eating Disorders*, April 2006.

larity of subjects with full-syndrome BN and EDNOS, however, may mitigate this limitation to some extent. . . .

Overall, the findings of the current study suggest that CBT, at least as adjusted for an adolescent population, deserves further evaluation. Early intervention with this age group could have a dramatic impact on the longer-term course of BN, potentially reducing chronicity and improving the quality of life for adolescents with eating disorders and their families.

"Insurance companies fail to cover all the necessary components of a successful treatment program."

Effective Treatment for Eating Disorders Depends on Increasing Insurance Coverage

Leah Litman

In the following viewpoint, Leah Litman argues that typical medical insurance plans are totally inadequate to successfully treat eating disorders. According to Litman, U.S. insurers cover only 10 percent of people diagnosed with eating disorders, and even this coverage falls far short of actual costs and duration of hospitalization, outpatient therapy, nutritional rehabilitation, and other necessary components of recovery. Without insurance coverage, Litman writes, sufferers forgo treatment or seek free, often inferior services, and eating disorders only get worse. Leah Litman, former editor in chief of the Harvard International Review *and presently a research assistant at the Washington, D.C., law firm Bancroft and Associates, enters Michigan Law School in August 2007.*

As you read, consider the following questions:

1. What is the difference between the amount of outpatient treatment typically covered by insurance companies and the amount of outpatient treatment necessary to effectively treat eating disorders, according to Litman?

2. Why does Litman argue that if lung cancer and sexually transmitted diseases are covered by medical insurers, eating disorders should be too?

3. How do insurers get around paying for eating disorder treatments, according to the author?

Today, we are bombarded with statistics and news stories about eating disorders. But the media have paid little attention to the treatment of eating disorders, despite the potential for significant national change in the upcoming months. The Mental Health Equitable Treatment Act (MHETA) [failed to pass Congress in 2003 and was reintroduced and failed again in 2005]. While MHETA takes the important first step of equating the seriousness of mental and physical illnesses, provisions in MHETA fail to adequately address the needs of eating disorder patients. While MHETA deals with all mental illnesses, it fails to adequately address the ambiguous place of eating disorders, which carry not only mental, but also physical and behavioral symptoms.

Eating Disorders Are Serious, Widespread Health Threats

Eating disorders are among the most prevalent and insidious mental illnesses. The Alliance for Eating Disorders Awareness has found that more than five million people in the United States suffer from either anorexia or bulimia. Medical data set the fatality rate of anorexia nervosa (intentional starvation accompanied by extreme weight loss) at ten percent, above that of any other psychological disorder. Anorexia contributes to cardiovascular diseases, which can lead to cardiac arrest; hematological illnesses, such as anemia; skeletal damage; and other medical complications. Other related eating disorders such as bulimia result in numerous gastrointestinal complications as extreme as stomach rupture. Not all eating disorders involve excessive weight loss. The American Obesity Association (AOA) has classified 60 million Americans as obese. Like other eating disorders, obesity carries severe health risks. AOA studies have linked obesity to high blood pressure, type II diabetes, heart disease, stroke, and gallbladder disease. Responding to these statistics, the Bush administration has undertaken publicity campaigns urging Americans to exercise. Because obesity has only recently been classified as an eating disorder, few improvements have been made in treating the psychological components of the disease.

Because social values promote dieting and thinness, eating disorders are difficult to diagnose. Moreover, these illnesses often remain undetected since many sufferers effectively conceal their symptoms. Eating disorders are also dangerous since the underlying psychological factors involved become progressively harder to address. But despite such well-established information, treatment for eating disorders is still difficult to obtain.

Insurers Are Permitted to Decide What to Pay For

Regulations at the federal and state level allow insurance providers to deny or provide only minimal coverage for eating-disorder patients. Before the Mental Health Parity Act of 1996 (MHPA), insurance companies were not bound to provide any treatment for mental illnesses. MHPA required coverage of mental illnesses but permitted insurance providers to cap the amount of coverage they would provide. MHPA also allowed insurance providers—not medical professionals—to determine how much coverage was necessary. Unfortunately, this assessment often leaves eating-disorder patients without adequate professional care. Insurance providers often determine the severity of the eating disorder based on the recurrence of the disease. However, research compiled by the Eating Disorders Coalition for Research Policy and Action indicates that the absence of early treatment often leads to relapses. Thus, by the time insurance companies decide to grant coverage, patients are often at a stage where they need the most intensive and expensive treatments with the lowest rates of success. Startling statistics—collected from insurance claims by Ruth Striegel-Moore, a psychologist at Wesleyan University—indicate that insurance companies only provide coverage for ten percent of people diagnosed with eating disorders. Despite diagnoses by health care professionals, insurance companies do not pay for their treatment.

The minimum coverage required under MHPA fails to encompass the range of treatment necessary for recovery. Hospitalization costs, which can run into the tens of thousands of dollars per month, are a primary component of treatment, and include nutritional rehabilitation and medical attention to many of the physical complications of eating disorders.

Hospitalization must be supplemented by various forms of therapy including nutritional and emotional counseling. Often, family members find counseling helpful in aiding their own understanding of eating disorders and in helping the patient's recovery.

Exclusions, Limitations, and Treatment Caps

Insurance companies fail to cover all the necessary components of a successful treatment program. The Eating Disorders Coalition for Research Policy and Action gathered data showing that insurance companies typically cover ten to fifteen sessions of outpatient treatment, while the American Psychiatric Association (APA) recommends forty sessions for patients identified even in the earlier stages of anorexia. Sometimes, insurance companies deny claims because patients have ex-

Case Studies Illustrate the Problem of Insurance Coverage for Eating Disorders

The National Eating Disorders Association (NEDA) fields thousands of questions each day. Many of them focus on how to gain access to care and navigate insurance issues. While there is little argument that early intervention offers the best chance for recovery, insurance often works as a barrier to prompt, thorough treatment....

Here are some stories that illustrate the problem:

Anna Westin was struggling with anorexia and needed intensive, specialized care. Her insurance company repeatedly denied this care stating that her treatment was "not medically necessary." Anna died from anorexia on February 17, 2000. Her parents joined the Minnesota Attorney General and sued the insurance company. The suit was settled out of court and the result has been greatly improved access to care for people with eating disorders and all mental health diagnoses in Minnesota....

Jane Doe* was diagnosed clinically anorexic by her therapist and recommended for inpatient treatment. Jane's insurance company repeatedly denied the inpatient treatment facility that Jane selected, stating that Jane needed to be treated by an "in-network" facility in her state. The problem was that none of the recommended insurance facilities treated eating disorders. The state also did not have an inpatient eating disorders treatment facility. After several denied appeals, Jane's insurance company did pay for 36 days of inpatient treatment, which was stated in her summary of benefits under the mental health section. The reimbursement was for about 50% of the total inpatient cost. (*Name changed for confidentiality.)

National Eating Disorders Association, "Insurance Issues,"
August 9, 2006.

ceeded their authorized number of treatments—even after the patient was initially approved for care and later hospitalized for relapse. The fiscal stipulations given to patients also fall short of estimated costs for treatment plans. The Ohio Department of Health estimates that the cost of outpatient treatment is around $30,000 and that inpatient treatment costs around $100,000 per incidence of the disease. Insurance providers often cap their coverage at $10,000 for outpatient care and $40,000 for inpatient care. This inadequate coverage forces patients either to forgo treatment or to pay the difference themselves, or to find other kinds of care. However, free services such as community-based support groups run by untrained caregivers are often inadequate. Several activist organizations have compiled stories of families that have bankrupted themselves to obtain the best care for family members.

Other insurance companies simply provide coverage for the physical aspects of the treatment and refuse to cover behavioral or psychological treatments. The patients are treated for physical complications such as malnutrition and dehydration, but coverage is not provided for nutritional counseling; psychopharmacology, such as antidepressants; or cognitive behavioral therapy. The patients then leave the hospital with only the symptoms and not the disease treated. According to the APA, those patients who only receive treatment for physical problems are just as likely to relapse as those who receive neither physical nor psychological treatment.

Insurers Overstate the Patient's Responsibility for Eating Disorders

Insurance companies have also been reluctant to cover weight-loss treatments for obese patients. Many insurance providers still classify obesity as a behavioral disorder—suggesting that the patient has complete personal responsibility for it—and therefore refuse to cover even the minimal treatment provided for in MHPA. However, even though certain behaviors do correlate to obesity, insurers cover other diseases associated with high-risk behavior. Smoking contributes to lung cancer, tanning contributes to skin cancer, and unprotected sex can lead to STDs, and yet insurance companies cover all of these diseases.

The role of personal responsibility in eating disorders is overstated and should not be an obstacle to insurance coverage. The treatments that insurance companies provide for obesity are usually limited to a few therapy sessions that are largely ineffective. However, other treatments may be more effective. In 1998, the National Institutes of Health (NIH) published recommendations for treating obese patients. These recommendations included physical treatments, such as surgery or pharmacology, in conjunction with therapy sessions to promote healthier lifestyles. The NIH guidelines also emphasize the importance of early intervention in treatment. Untreated patients are more likely to experience medical complications associated with obesity and their long-term psychological problems are more difficult to treat.

Removing Barriers to Treatment

The mental health parity outlined in MHETA is a first step toward achieving obtainable care for eating disorders. Under MHETA, several barriers in the way of treatment are to be removed. MHETA mandates that insurance companies remove co-payment requirements for mental illnesses. MHETA also eliminates the predetermined limits set on treatments. . . .

Unfortunately, many of the shortcomings of MHPA have found their way into MHETA, which still allows insurance companies a large amount of discretion to determine who is truly "mentally ill" and eligible for coverage. In concessions to the insurance industry, policymakers have allowed arbitrary exclusions and treatment limitations to be incorporated into MHETA. For instance, MHETA explicitly says that insurance companies make the final treatment decisions.

The potential failures of the act are evident in several state parity laws that have already been enacted. Thirty-four states have passed parity laws similar to the pending congressional legislation. However, the National Association for Anorexia Nervosa and Associated Disorders points to the fact that [in all but twelve states as of December 2006], eating disorders are not [mandated] because insurance companies claim that eating disorders are not exclusively a mental illness. Insurance companies refuse to provide coverage for eating disorders on the grounds that they are behavioral illnesses, which do not fall under mental health parity guidelines.

The federal legislation provides one additional loophole for insurance companies. Unlike the many state laws, MHETA does not require insurance companies to provide mental health care. Even though it removes co-payment requirements and arbitrary limits on the number of therapy sessions, patients only reap those benefits if the insurance company decides to cover treatment, effectively nullifying any positive effect of MHETA. Moreover, MHETA does not address whether eating disorders are mental illnesses or behavioral diseases brought on by the patient's lifestyle. Therefore, insurance companies can continue to deny coverage by making this arbitrary distinction.

Coverage for College Students Is Sorely Needed

While many insurance companies provide minimal coverage, others have instituted a degree of parity even in the absence of such a legal requirement. The insurance coverage offered through Harvard University Health Services (UHS) offers unlimited care from physicians, nutritionists, and psychologists. Services offered through Harvard also include numerous counseling and support groups for patients suffering from eating disorders and for those who are close to them. The Bureau of Study Counsel also offers individual and group counseling for those with eating concerns. Although long-term medical treatment can be limited by availability, insurance coverage for care provided by UHS is unlimited. The elective Blue Cross Blue Shield plan also covers twelve mental health visits to doctors outside of UHS and three other medical visits to doctors not affiliated with UHS who specialize in non-mental illnesses.

Because adolescents and young adults are at high risk for eating disorders, coverage for college students is incredibly important. A 1987 study at George Mason University reports that five to twenty percent of college women are either anorexic or bulimic. Although the level of coverage at Harvard is not available at all schools, many universities have been making efforts to improve health care for eating disorders. For instance, Wellesley increased its coverage so group therapy sessions are now covered under the university health insurance program.

Every person deserves to have access to quality care, especially in a time of need. Even the proposed changes to mental health's status under insurance guidelines are inadequate to help those suffering from eating disorders. Instead, they allow insurance companies to deny sufficient care rather than providing patients with the full range of treatment options that can help them overcome an eating disorder.

Periodical Bibliography

The following articles have been selected to supplement the diverse views presented in this chapter.

| American Dietetic Association | "Position of the ADA: Nutrition Intervention in the Treatment of Anorexia Nervosa, Bulimia Nervosa, and Other Eating Disorders," *Journal of the American Dietetic Association*, December 2006, pp. 2073–82. |

B. Bower — "Starved for Assistance: Coercion Finds a Place in the Treatment of Two Eating Disorders," *Science News*, January 20, 2007, p. 38.

Lauren Brown — "21 Days to Save Her Life," *CosmoGirl!* February 2007, pp. 116–20.

Jennifer Couturier and James Lock — "What Is Recovery in Adolescent Anorexia Nervosa?" *International Journal of Eating Disorders*, vol. 39, no. 7, November 2006, pp. 550–55.

James Greenblatt and Stuart Koman — "Treat Eating Disorders Concurrently: Treatment Will Require Intensive Monitoring at the Outset," *Addiction Professional*, July/August 2006, pp. 43–46.

Timothy F. Kirn — "Fluoxetine Offers No Benefit for Anorexia Patients," *Clinical Psychiatry News*, August 2006, p. 67.

Matthew Lynn — "Too Fat, Too Thin? Let People Decide Their Own Weight," *Bloomberg.com*, December 20, 2006. www.bloomberg.com.

Mayo Clinic — "Family-Based Therapy for Anorexia Nervosa," *Clinical Update*, February 21, 2005.

Catherine Soban — "What About the Boys? Addressing Issues of Masculinity Within Male Anorexia Nervosa in a Feminist Therapeutic Environment," *International Journal of Men's Health*, vol. 5, no. 3, Fall 2006, pp. 251–67.

For Further Discussion

Chapter 1

1. The Eating Disorders Coalition for Research, Policy & Action describes eating disorders as endemic and underreported across all demographic groups in the United States. Malcolm Evans argues that such claims, and even the labeling of behaviors as pathological, inevitably make people see disease where none exists. What factual evidence, not opinions, do these authors present to support their arguments?

2. Anne Iverson maintains that black women are generally more satisfied with their bodies than white women, and less susceptible to eating disorders in part because images of black women in the mass media tend to be positive, fuller-figured, and realistic and images of white women are more often ultrathin and unattainable. Denise Brodey argues that minority women feel the same pressure to conform to idealized media images as white women, and only *seem* less susceptible to eating disorders because they are far less likely to come forward or seek treatment. Which author makes the stronger argument? Support your answer with examples based on your own television and film-viewing habits.

3. Susan Z. Yanovski suggests that eating disorders are a cause of the epidemic of obesity in the United States. Courtney E. Martin suggests, on the contrary, that exaggerated claims of an obesity epidemic cause eating disorders. Are these cause-and-effect claims mutually exclusive? If not, how could both claims be true?

Chapter 2

1. Craig Johnson and Cynthia Bulik, Randy Schellenberg, and Ellen Ruppel Shell all suggest that eating disorders have physiological rather than psychiatric causes. On what points do the authors agree? What are their main differences?

2. Janet Treasure, a physician and the director of an eating disorders treatment facility, says skeletally thin fashion models trigger EDs in vulnerable young patients and the fashion industry should be held accountable. Michelle Cottle, an editor at a politically conservative magazine, opposes government regulation of the fashion industry as unjustified meddling. How might these authors' professional positions affect their objectivity on this issue?

Chapter 3

1. Elanor Taylor argues that pro-ana Web sites should be shut down because they present dangerously disordered behaviors as normal. Angie Rankman argues that pro-ana Web sites should *not* be shut down because they present dangerously disordered behaviors as normal. How do these authors use the same evidence to draw opposite conclusions?

2. Kristen Depowski and Kelly Hart are legal researchers who describe the design and content of pro-ED Web sites as slickly packaged propaganda that entices visitors into agreeing with their point of view. How might the authors' backgrounds affect their viewpoint on this issue?

3. Theresia Laksmana describes anonymity and accessibility as reasons why the Internet can be a positive tool in the treatment of eating disorders. Suggest ways in which these factors might also hinder ED treatment online. In your opinion, do the advantages outweigh the disadvantages? Why or why not?

Chapter 4

1. James L. Werth Jr. makes a case for involuntary hospitalization and, if necessary, force feeding, of anorexics based on a physician's duty to protect patients. Simona Giordano maintains, on the contrary, that in some cases individual autonomy must be respected, and compulsory treatment would be unethical. Which author do you believe makes the more persuasive argument, and why?

2. James Lock promotes family therapy, based on close family monitoring of meals and active, nonjudgmental family intervention, as the best known treatment for anorexia. Judith Graham actually quotes Lock, however, to support her argument that there are no effective treatments for anorexia. Compare Lock's statements in both articles, then discuss whether or not they are in fact contradictory.

3. Ann M. Schapman-Williams, James Lock, and Jennifer Couturier support cognitive-behavioral therapy for bulimia and binge eating disorder, while Diane Mickley argues that medication is most promising. Though they are discussing the same disorders, the authors are actually tailoring their treatment preferences to different patient populations. Based on evidence from the viewpoints, suggest reasons why different treatments might be indicated for different groups.

4. How would the Mental Health Equitable Treatment Act remove barriers to eating disorder treatment, according to Leah Litman?

Organizations to Contact

The editors have compiled the following list of organizations concerned with the issues debated in this book. The descriptions are derived from materials provided by the organizations. All have publications or information available for interested readers. The list was compiled on the date of publication of the present volume; the information provided here may change. Be aware that many organizations take several weeks or longer to respond to inquiries, so allow as much time as possible.

Academy for Eating Disorders (AED)
60 Revere Dr., Suite 500, Northbrook, IL 60062-1577
e-mail: info@aedweb.org
Web site: www.aedweb.org

The AED is an international organization of eating disorder research, treatment, and education professionals. It fosters education, training, and interdisciplinary dialogue; holds an annual conference; and develops guidelines for clinical treatment practices. For the general public, the Web site offers archives of AED press releases and position statements and information about research study participation and locating treatment providers. Eight times a year, the AED publishes the *International Journal of Eating Disorders*, containing full-length scholarly articles, reviews, brief reports, case reports, research, and clinical forums addressing the psychological, biological, sociocultural, epidemiological, and therapeutic aspects of eating disorders. Abstracts of journal contents since 1996 are online at www3.interscience.wiley.com/cgi-bin/jhome/34698; full articles may be downloaded with purchase.

Anorexia Nervosa and Related Eating Disorders, Inc. (ANRED)
e-mail: jarinor@rio.com
Web site: www.anred.com

ANRED is a nonprofit organization based in California that maintains an online clearinghouse for information on eating disorders. Cofounded by ED specialist Jean Bradley Rubel, clinical psychologist Susannah Smith, and colleagues, ANRED compiles accurate, up-to-date information on EDs including statistics, warning signs, incidence, effects, and complications. The site offers links to research studies and trials, educational conferences and workshops, FAQs, and related Web sites; a bibliography for clinicians and general readers; and a forum for posting personal experience with eating disorders. ANRED responds confidentially to e-mail inquiries but does not make treatment referrals.

Eating Disorder Referral and Information Center (EDRIC)
2923 Sandy Pointe, Suite 6, Del Mar, CA   92014-2052
(858) 792-7463 • fax: (775) 261-9364
Web site: www.edreferral.com

EDRIC offers a useful online database of information on many aspects of eating disorders, including ED definitions, body image issues, at-risk groups, compulsive overeating, and treatment options. The company also offers a membership directory of treatment providers; please note that EDRIC does not verify listees' licenses, credentials, services, or any other claim. Thus, people seeking help for an eating disorder must not consider these referrals trustworthy without independently and carefully checking their qualifications.

**Eating Disorders Coalition for Research,
Policy & Action (EDC)**
611 Pennsylvania Ave. SE, #423
Washington, DC   20003-4303
(202) 543-9570
e-mail: manager@eatingdisorderscoalition.org
Web site: www.eatingdisorderscoalition.org

The EDC is a nonprofit association of leading eating disorder advocacy groups, research programs, and treatment facilities that seek federal recognition of eating disorders as a public health priority, more federal funding for research and treatment, and parity in insurance coverage for mental and physical health services. EDC activities focus on influencing members of Congress and other policy makers through briefings and education, support of legislation, and petition drives. At the EDC Web site, the general public can view reports about pending legislation and health insurance issues; sign up for e-mail updates; and get involved in EDC activities through the EDC Family & Friends Action Council.

Food and Nutrition Information Center
National Agricultural Library
10301 Baltimore Ave., Room 105, Beltsville, MD 20705
(301) 504-5414 • fax: (301) 504-6409
e-mail: fnic@nal.usda.gov
Web site: http://fnic.nal.usda.gov

This section of the U.S. Department of Agriculture offers a Diet and Disease, Eating Disorders Web site that includes many links to resource material on anorexia, bulimia, and binge eating; exercise and eating disorders; teens and eating disorders; and dietary and nutrition assistance programs.

Gürze Books
5145 B Avenida Encinas, Carlsbad, CA 92008
(800) 756-7533
e-mail: kelli@gurze.net
Web site: www.gurze.com

Gürze is an independent, California-based publisher specializing in eating disorders publications and education since 1980. The company offers a free eating-disorders resource catalog listing books and tapes from over fifty publishers as well as its own publications; a bimonthly newsletter for clinicians, the *Eating Disorders Review*; a quarterly newsletter for the general public, *Eating Disorders Today*; and a quarterly Internet newsletter, *Gürze E-News*.

National Association of Anorexia Nervosa and Associated Disorders (ANAD)

(847) 831-3438 • fax: (847) 433-4632
e-mail: anad20@aol.com
Web site: www.anad.org

ANAD is a national, nonprofit, largely volunteer organization based in Highland Park, Illinois, founded in 1976 to raise awareness of eating disorders and to promote treatment and recovery. ANAD representatives help sufferers and their families through hotline counseling and online referrals to support groups and treatment professionals. The ANAD Web site includes links to information about specific disorders, pending legislation, event schedules, and the organization's online newsletter (services are free but registration is required for treatment referrals).

National Eating Disorders Association (NEDA)

603 Stewart St., Suite 803, Seattle, WA   98101
(206) 382-3587
e-mail: info@NationalEatingDisorders.org
Web site: www.edap.org

Formed in 2001 by the merger of Eating Disorders Awareness & Prevention (EDAP) and the American Anorexia Bulimia Association (AABA), NEDA is the largest nonprofit group in the United States dedicated to eating disorder education, treatment, and prevention. The association provides a toll-free information and referral helpline; sponsors an annual conference for families, educators, and treatment providers; awards research grants; and lobbies legislators to expand public education programs and patient access to treatment facilities. A comprehensive index of free fact sheets is available at the Web site, and NEDA's online store sells educational videos, books, brochures, posters, and promotional items.

National Institute of Mental Health (NIMH)

Public Information and Communications Branch
Bethesda, MD   20892-9663

toll-free: (866) 615-6464 • fax: (301) 443-4279
e-mail: nimhinfo@nih.gov
Web site: www.nimh.nih.gov

The institute, a branch of the National Institutes of Health within the U.S. Department of Health and Human Services, is the lead federal agency for research on mental and behavioral disorders, including eating disorders. Its most recent publication on the topic, the 2001 booklet "Eating Disorders: Facts About Eating Disorders and the Search for Solutions," is available to read or download free of charge at www.nimh.nih.gov/publicat/eatingdisorders.cfm. More recent, brief news articles about eating disorders are posted periodically at the Web site's Press Room section, and good descriptions of current government-sponsored eating-disorder research studies (including patient recruitment information) are listed at the site's Clinical Trials section.

Renfrew Center Foundation
475 Spring Lane, Philadelphia, PA 19128
(877) 367-3383 • fax: (215) 482-2695
e-mail: foundation@renfrew.org
Web site: www.renfrew.org

The foundation is a nonprofit education and research organization, founded in 1990 by the Renfrew Center, the nation's first free-standing facility exclusively dedicated to the treatment of eating disorders. To raise public awareness, the foundation conducts educational seminars, sponsors a speakers bureau, and has launched a sticker campaign targeting ads and articles that promote eating disorders. The foundation's Web site offers abundant resource material, including action guides and bibliographies of recommended books; educational flyers, posters, quizzes, CD-ROMs, and videos; a free newsletter, *Connections*; and a biannual professional journal, *Perspectives*.

Something Fishy Website on Eating Disorders
Web site: www.something-fishy.org

Something Fishy is a highly regarded Internet eating-disorder support and information site founded in 1995 and owned since 2006 by CRC Health Group of Cupertino, California. The site is dedicated to raising awareness of eating disorders, moderating an interactive community of people with eating disorders and their loved ones, and constructively promoting recovery. Resources include peer support forums and bulletin boards; an online treatment finder; news articles; and links to related organizations, hotlines, and research and educational material. As a pro-recovery site, Something Fishy opposes Web sites that portray eating disorders as a "normal" lifestyle choice, and members/visitors are not allowed to post pictures, advice, or discussion that might trigger disordered behaviors, such as calorie counts, body-mass index calculations, weight-loss tips, or photographs of thin models and celebrities.

Bibliography of Books

Arnold Andersen, Leigh Cohn, and Thomas Holbrook — *Making Weight*. Carlsbad, CA: Gürze, 2000.

Robin F. Apple and W. Stewart Agras — *Overcoming Eating Disorders: A Cognitive-Behavioral Treatment for Bulimia Nervosa and Binge-Eating Disorder Workbook*. 2nd. ed. New York: Oxford University Press, 2007.

Katherine A. Beals — *Disordered Eating Among Athletes: A Comprehensive Guide for Health Professionals*. Champaign, IL: Human Kinetics, 2004.

Thomas F. Cash and Thomas Pruzinsky, eds. — *Body Image: A Handbook of Theory, Research & Clinical Practice*. New York: Guilford, 2004.

Laura Collins — *Eating with Your Anorexic*. New York: McGraw-Hill, 2004.

Myra Cooper — *The Psychology of Bulimia Nervosa: A Cognitive Perspective*. New York: Oxford University Press, 2006.

Cheryl Dellasega — *The Starving Family: Caregiving Mothers and Fathers Share Their Eating Disorder Wisdom*. Belgium, WI: Champion, 2005.

Nancy Etcoff — *Survival of the Prettiest: The Science of Beauty*. New York: Anchor, 2000.

Christopher G. Fairburn and Kelly D. Brownell, eds. — *Eating Disorders and Obesity: A Comprehensive Handbook*. 2nd ed. New York: Guilford, 2005.

Lauren Greenfield — *Thin*. San Francisco: Chronicle, 2006.

Jeanne Albronda Heaton and Claudia J. Strauss — *Talking to Eating Disorders: Simple Ways to Support Someone with Anorexia, Bulimia, Binge Eating, or Body Image Issues*. New York: NAL Trade, 2005.

Jennifer Hendricks — *Slim to None: A Journey Through the Wasteland of Anorexia Treatment*. New York: McGraw-Hill, 2003.

Sharlene Hesse-Biber — *The Cult of Thinness*. 2nd ed. New York: Oxford University Press, 2006.

Marya Hornbacher — *Wasted: A Memoir of Anorexia and Bulimia (P.S.)*. New York: HarperPerennial, 2006.

Jo Kingsley and Alice Kingsley — *Alice in the Looking Glass: A Mother and Daughter's Experience of Anorexia*. London: Piatkus, 2005.

Carolyn Kitch — *The Girl on the Magazine Cover: The Origins of Visual Stereotypes in American Mass Media*. Chapel Hill: University of North Carolina Press, 2000.

Karen R. Koenig — *The Rules of "Normal" Eating: A Commonsense Approach for Dieters, Overeaters, Undereaters, Emotional Eaters, and Everyone in Between*. Carlsbad, CA: Gürze, 2005.

Nancy Kolodny — *Beginner's Guide to ED Recovery.* Carlsbad, CA: Gürze, 2004.

Chris Kraatz — *Radical Recovery: A Manifesto of Eating Disorder Pride.* Lanham, MD: University Press of America, 2006.

Jenny Langley — *Boys Get Anorexia Too: Coping with Male Eating Disorders in the Family.* London: Paul Chapman, 2006.

Daniel Le Grange and James Lock — *Treating Bulimia in Adolescents: A Family-Based Approach.* New York: Guilford, 2007.

Aimee Liu — *Gaining: The Truth About Life After Eating Disorders.* New York: Warner, 2007.

James Lock and Daniel Le Grange — *Help Your Teenager Beat an Eating Disorder.* New York: Guilford, 2004.

Richard Maisel, David Epston, and Ali Borden — *Biting the Hand That Starves You: Inspiring Resistance to Anorexia/Bulimia.* New York: W. W. Norton, 2004.

Beverly Neu Menassa — *Preventing Eating Disorders Among Pre-Teen Girls: A Step-by-Step Guide.* New York: Praeger, 2004.

James E. Mitchell and Carol B. Peterson, eds. — *Assessment of Eating Disorders.* New York: Guilford, 2005.

Mervat Nasser, Melanie A. Katzman, and Richard A. Gordon, eds. — *Eating Disorders and Cultures in Transition.* Leicester, UK: Brunner-Routledge, 2002.

Anna Paterson   *Fit to Die: Men and Eating Disorders.* London: Paul Chapman, 2004.

Gary Stromberg and Jane Merrill   *Feeding the Fame: Celebrities Tell Their Real-Life Stories of Eating Disorders and Recovery.* Ontario: Hazelden, 2006.

Janet Treasure, Grainne Smith, and Anna Crane   *Skills-Based Learning for Caring for a Loved One with an Eating Disorder: The New Maudsley Method.* London: Routledge, 2007.

Eda. R Uca   *Ana's Girls: The Essential Guide to the Underground Eating Disorder Community Online.* Bloomington, IN: AuthorHouse, 2004.

Maggie Wykes and Barrie Gunter   *The Media and Body Image: If Looks Could Kill.* Thousand Oaks, CA: Sage, 2005.

Index